# Teaching with Words in Color

*Lesson Guides, Techniques, Games*

---
## American English Edition
---

Educational Solutions Worldwide Inc.

Copyright © 2009 Educational Solutions Worldwide Inc.
Second Edition
Based on the works of Dr. Caleb Gattegno, including: Notes For Parents, ©1979
Compiled by Educational Solutions Worldwide Inc.
All rights reserved
ISBN 978-0-87825-154-4

Educational Solutions Worldwide Inc.
2nd Floor 99 University Place, New York, N.Y. 10003-4555
www.EducationalSolutions.com

# Table of Contents

Introduction .................................................................................1

$R_0$ The First Group of Activities ...............................................15

$R_1$ The Second Group of Activities ..........................................27

$R_2$, $R_3$ and Beyond ...............................................................79

Words in Color Toolbox ..............................................................83

      Teaching Techniques ......................................................87

      Games ..........................................................................109

- 1 Fidel Phonic Code™ (size varies depending on set)
- 21 color-coded Word Charts (size varies depending on set)
- Color Key for the American English Fidel™
- Reference Guide to the Fidel Phonic Code™
- Reading Primers $R_0$ & $R_1$
- Reading Primer $R_2$
- Reading Primer $R_3$
- Student Workbook 1
- Student Workbook 2
- Book of Stories
- Teaching with Words in Color
- Collapsible metal pointer

# Introduction

# The Challenge

Spelling 1: e as in pet
Spelling 2: ea as in lead
Spelling 3: a as in any
Spelling 4: u as in bury
Spelling 5: ai as in said
Spelling 6: ay as in says
Spelling 7: ie as in friend
Spelling 8: eo as in leopard
Spelling 9: ei as in heifer
Spelling 10: ae as in aesthetic

One sound can have many spellings.

English is a non-phonetic language riddled with ambiguities. Although the alphabet has just 26 letters, we use many more than 26 sounds in our speech. In fact, American-English speakers use about 59 sounds depending on dialect.

The first major ambiguity of English is that there are often many ways to spell the same sound – sometimes dozens of ways. For example, consider the 10 ways of spelling the sound e as in pet, as pictured above. The second ambiguity is that a single spelling can be pronounced in several ways. For example, imagine the eight different ways to pronounce the letter 'e.'

Sound 1: e as in English
Sound 2: e as in pet
Sound 3: e as in the
Sound 4: e as in her
Sound 5: e as in sergeant
Sound 6: e as in we
Sound 7: e as in there
Sound 8: e as in suede

This is very confusing for beginning readers because letters only show how a word is spelled, not how it is pronounced.

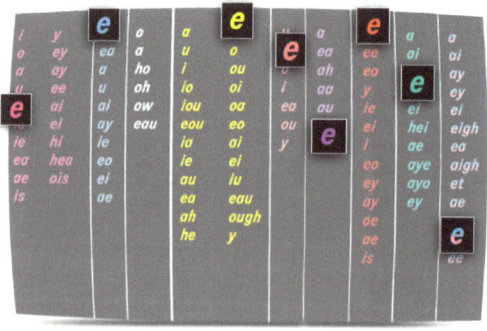

One spelling can produce many sounds.

# The Solutions

The first solution to the problem of ambiguities is color. With Words in Color, each of the 59 sounds in English is assigned a unique color, and all 400+ spellings are organized by sound. Color provides students with a logical, phonetic basis for decoding and reading specific words.

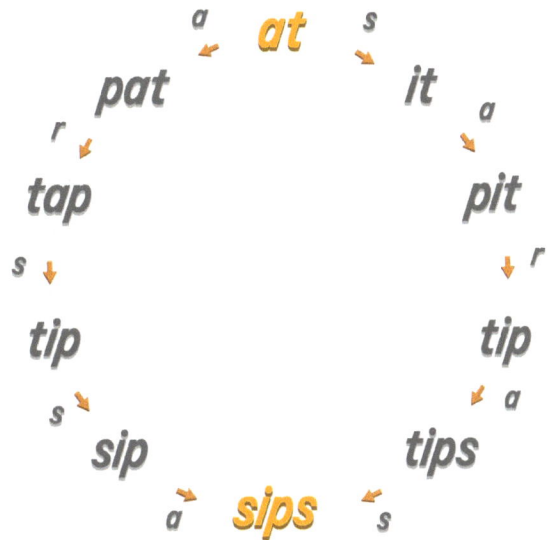

The Transformation Game uses algebraic operations.

The second solution is using the algebraic nature of English. Letters, syllables and words can be combined in many different ways. By placing emphasis on the processes for combining these elements, we set the stage for significant acceleration in learning outcomes.

For example, starting with the sounds and spellings in the word pat, we can generate the words tap and apt just by combining the sounds differently. If we add s as in stop, e as in pet, and o as in pot to the mix, we can generate 39 words. Rather than teach these 39 words individually, the Words in Color approach teaches students about processes for combining the 6 sounds. This way students can discover and create new combinations by themselves without memorizing. The Transformation Game, found on page 118-119, uses the algebraic processes of addition, reversal, insertion and substitution to transform one word into another. Students have a lot of fun playing, and also discover the relationships between sounds.

# The Materials

The American English Fidel ™

## The Fidel™

The American English Fidel ™ is your guide through the language. The Fidel™, an Ethiopian word meaning alphabet, presents all the 400+ ways of spelling the 59 sounds in English. Color is applied to help beginning readers know how to read a word. For example, when we apply color to the words <u>fruit</u>, <u>flu</u>, and <u>food</u>, we provide conditions that enable students to become aware that in this case <u>ui</u>, <u>u</u>, and <u>oo</u> (in dark green) are all to be read with the same sound, even though the spellings are different.

pat pit pet pot
pop at it up putt
tot top tip tap apt
as pep us pup is
-s sat sit set sap -s
's stop step spot 's
stops steps pass pest
sips tess tests past
puppet asset

21 Color-Coded Word Charts

## Word Charts

A graded set of 21 colored word charts introduces students through carefully selected examples to the spectrum of spellings for each sound, and how to decode them. The words chosen at each level are first those most useful in sentence formation and progress from easier, to common usage, to difficult and uncommon examples.

Continued . . .

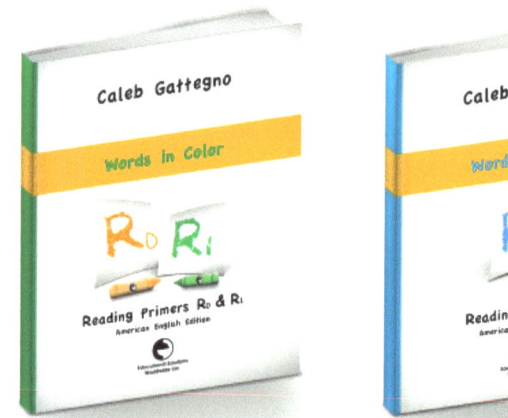 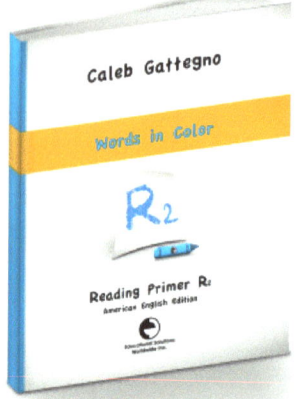 

Reading Primers $R_0$ & $R_1$, $R_2$, $R_3$

## Reading Primers

The student Reading Primers introduce in stages all the different spellings and sounds of American English, giving examples of words, and of their use in sentences. They are printed in black and white and are written for use in conjunction with the Fidel™ and the Words in Color set of 21 Word Charts. They provide a detailed progression for classroom and home work and eliminate dependence on color for reading.

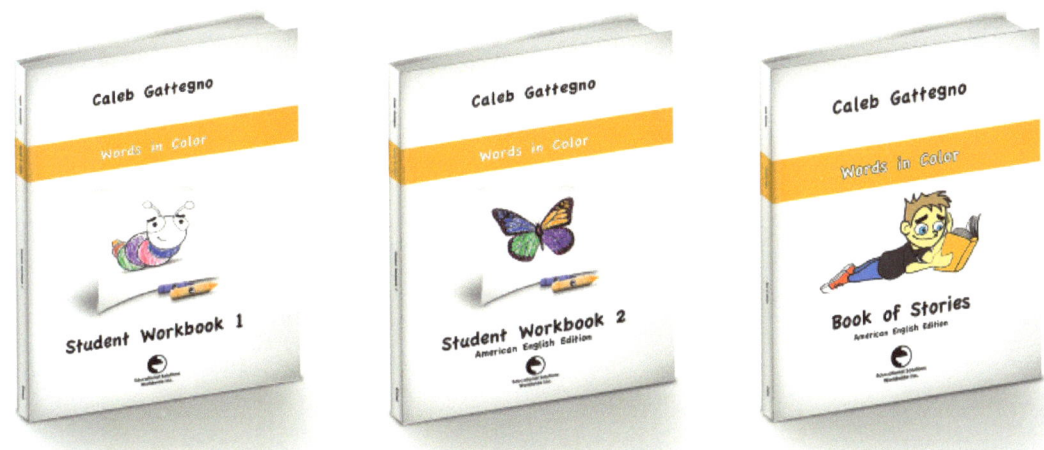

Student Workbook 1, Student Workbook 2, Book of Stories

## Workbooks

Each Workbook contains 7 multi-page worksheets with graduated questions and exercises to consolidate the reading skills at each stage. They provide a program of individual study where imagination and creativity are encouraged, with a proven framework for their expression. The worksheets progress from the beginning of reading and writing through to an introductory study of grammar.

## Book of Stories

Specially written for use with Words in Color, 40 stories describe events in the daily lives of an everyday family. As the first continuous reading material students meet, this book takes into account the increasing complexity of written English as presented on the Fidel™, the set of 21 color-coded Word Charts, and the Reading Primers.

Continued . . .

Reference Guide to the Fidel Phonic Code ™, Color Key for the American English Fidel ™

## Reference Guide to the Fidel™

This is a comprehensive resource that presents sample words and their corresponding locations on the Word Charts for every sound and spelling on the Fidel™.

## Color Key

This is a quick reference to all the sounds, spellings, and colors on the Fidel™.

Teaching with Words in Color

# This Guide

Teaching With Words in Color is for teachers and parents who are new to the approach. This guide provides a general introduction to the materials, and takes the first time instructor through $R_0$ and $R_1$. It also provides a toolbox of games and teaching techniques that can be used at any stage.

## Additional Resources

Visit the Words in Color section at www.EducationalSolutions.com for updates, instructional videos, and additional resources on how to use and apply Words in Color.

# Frequently Asked Questions

## Do I have to start from the beginning if my student already has some reading skills?

It is not necessary, however, some users have found that when you start from the first lessons, students start to understand the foundations of the English language. More challenging words will become easier to read and spell since they have the inherent knowledge. It has been found that the pace of learning in subsequent lessons is often accelerated when you start from the beginning.

## What if my pronunciation is not the same as the color indicates?

The pronunciations of words chosen for Words in Color are consistent with those as presented in The American Heritage Dictionary, Fourth Edition. However, we understand there are many regional dialects of American English and that each region of the continent has its own way of pronouncing certain sounds. For example, the sign o in the word pop found in Chart 1 may be pronounced differently by someone in Boston, Massachusetts versus someone in Dallas, Texas and someone in Minneapolis, Minnesota. And this may be different again from the form of English spoken in Chicago, Illinois.

We encourage you to pronounce the sounds (and their associated color) as you normally would. In fact, depending on the region you live in, there may be no distinction between the pronunciations associated with certain colors. For example, the o (colored white) as in the word pop and the o (colored ochre) as in the word off may be pronounced the same in the dialect of English spoken where you live.

By all means, use the dialect of English that you use naturally. This program is about learning to read, not learning to pronounce. Treat this an opportunity to explore the richness of the English language – one that has taken centuries to develop.

## Where are the capital letters? Is this a mistake?

Capital letters and punctuation have intentionally been omitted for the beginning stages of reading and writing. If your child or student already knows about capitals, then they will automatically apply that knowledge. If they do not know about these conventions, it is better to wait until they have a grasp of the basics before complicating matters with different shapes (capitals) for the same signs.

## How much time should I spend on this at home?

Introducing a sound, or playing a game can take just two minutes. You can keep playing the games and increasing the challenges for as long as your student is interested. For very young children, you may find you have more success if you use Words in Color more frequently, but for shorter periods of time. Be aware of the interest level in your student; if they are ready to do something else after five minutes, then five minutes is enough. If they are very interested in a game, keep playing and keep increasing the challenge. If you spend one hour on an activity, and the student is only interested for 20 minutes, then 40 minutes of the lesson may not have been effective. Think quality, not quantity.

# Before You Begin

## Get Familiar with the Fidel

Take out your full-size Fidel and examine it. What do you notice?

Refer to the Reference Guide to the Fidel Phonic Code and the Color Key for the American English Fidel for sample words and official color names.

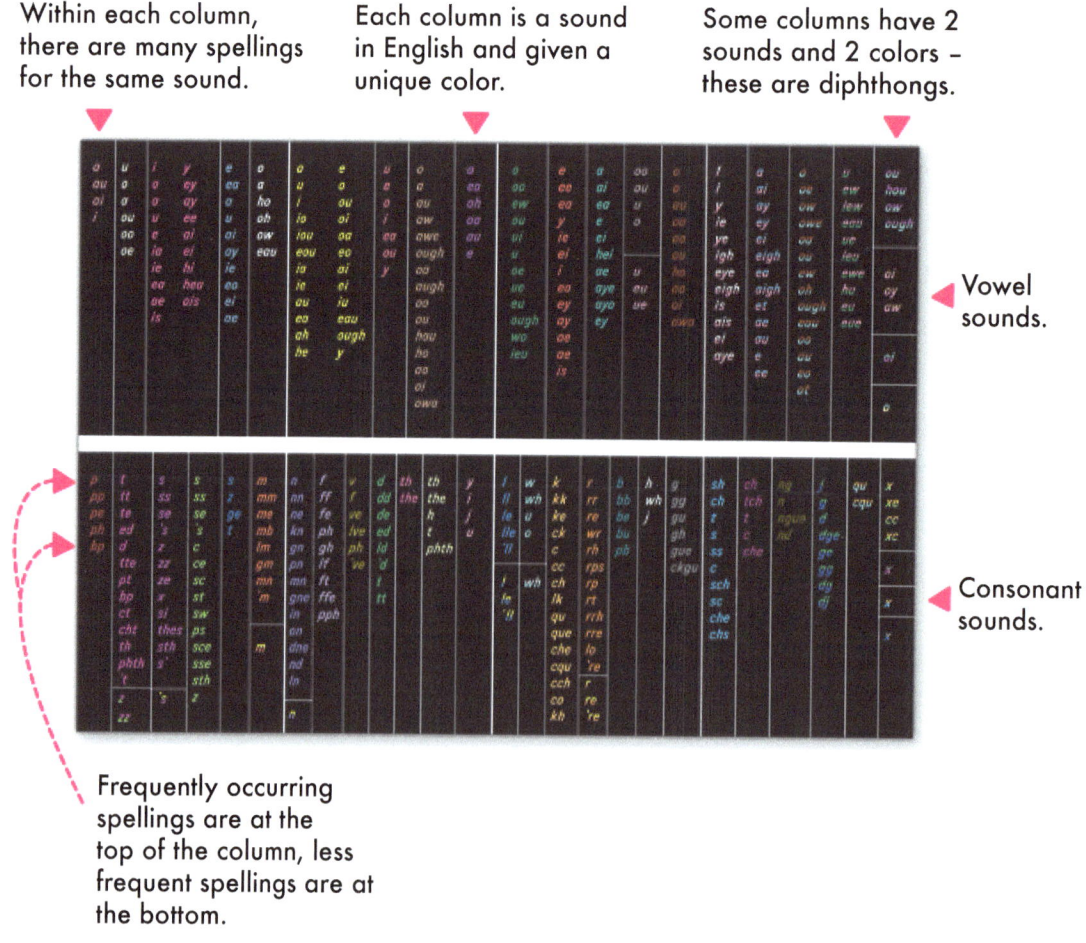

Within each column, there are many spellings for the same sound.

Each column is a sound in English and given a unique color.

Some columns have 2 sounds and 2 colors – these are diphthongs.

◀ Vowel sounds.

◀ Consonant sounds.

Frequently occurring spellings are at the top of the column, less frequent spellings are at the bottom.

## Get REALLY Familiar with English Sounds & Spellings

The following activities are designed to make you more familiar with the use of the materials. We have found that going through these activities, in whole or in part is very beneficial for the teacher. It is not necessary to complete each one before you begin. You can always return to these as you progress.

..........................................................................................

*Activity 1*
Start at word chart #1. For each word on the first row, say it and:
- Find the matching color and spelling on the Fidel Phonic Code
- Continue until you have finished all the words on the row
- Repeat the process for the next line

..........................................................................................

*Activity 2*
Start at the first sound/spelling on the top left of the Fidel Phonic Code.
For each sound/spelling:
Can you find any/all instances of its use on the word charts? How many did you find?

..........................................................................................

## Continued . . .

*Activity 3*
In each Reading Primer ($R_0$ & $R_1$, $R_2$, $R_3$), find the Word Building Tables 0-7. Starting with Table 1, find the corresponding sounds and spellings on the Fidel Phonic Code. After you have finished, proceed to the next Word Building Table.

. . . . . . . . . . . . . . . . . . . . . . . . . . . . . . . . . . . . . . . . . . . . . . . . . . . . . . . . . . . . . . . . .

*Activity 4*
Starting with Reading Primer $R_0$ & $R_1$, read each word and sentence. Can you find words in the Reading Primer book that are also written on the Word Charts? After you have finished one Reading Primer, proceed to the next.

. . . . . . . . . . . . . . . . . . . . . . . . . . . . . . . . . . . . . . . . . . . . . . . . . . . . . . . . . . . . . . . . .

*Activity 5*
Starting with Worksheet 1 in Student Workbook 1:
- Identify the spellings and sounds that are in use.
- Find the corresponding locations for the sounds and spellings on the Fidel.

. . . . . . . . . . . . . . . . . . . . . . . . . . . . . . . . . . . . . . . . . . . . . . . . . . . . . . . . . . . . . . . . .

# $R_0$
# The First Group of Activities

# Overview of $R_0$

In the $R_0$ portion of Reading Primers $R_0$ & $R_1$ you will work on the following sounds:

This initial table is made of five vowel sounds:
- <u>a</u> as in <u>a</u>t
- <u>u</u> as in <u>u</u>p
- <u>i</u> as in <u>i</u>t
- <u>e</u> as in p<u>e</u>t
- <u>o</u> as in p<u>o</u>t

At this stage you will also be making your student aware of some conventions of written English:
- The text is to be read from left to right.
- There are spaces between the words.
- Signs, alone, or in groups represent sounds.

Keep in mind, you won't tell the student these conventions. Let them discover for themself.

# Table 0.1 Activity 1

### Sound / Spelling
- <u>a</u> as in p<u>a</u>t

### Materials
- Chart 0
- Reading Primers $R_0$ & $R_1$
- Pointer

## Beginning Notes

In our approach to teaching reading, we refer to sounds and not letters. The rationale is that there are only 26 letters in English, but they produce 59 sounds. Combinations of the 5 vowels alone create 23 sounds with hundreds of spellings – this is a great source of confusion for learners. Using the name of a letter creates an incomplete notion of the letter's pronunciation, and makes it difficult for learners to accept new spellings.

Rather than refer to letters, we refer to sounds. For example, the sound associated with <u>p</u> as in <u>p</u>at can be referred to by the sound/color chestnut, and <u>s</u> as in u<u>s</u> can be called lime green. Refer to the Color Key for the American English Fidel for a complete list of the official names for all 59 sounds.

If you give the time and support for your child or student to work through and conquer the challenges presented, they will become better prepared to meet even bigger, more complex challenges. Remember:

- Resist the temptation to give answers.
- Allow your student time to work through and conquer challenges.
- Repetition can be detrimental to the learning process. Thus, try to mix up the challenges if your student is "not getting it."
- If difficulties arise, revert back to what is already known and go from there.

# Table 0.1 Activity 1

## Steps

- Using your pointer, point to <u>a</u> on Chart 0 and say its sound once. Remember you are not naming a letter of the alphabet, you are using the sound <u>a</u> as in p<u>a</u>t.
- Point to another <u>a</u> and ask your student to say the sound.
- Point to each sign in "<u>aa</u>" and ask your student to say the sounds. If they cannot say these sounds then say it once and ask them to say it.
- Point to each spelling (sign) in "<u>aaa</u>" and ask your student to say the sounds. If they cannot say these sounds then say it once and ask them to say it.
- Switch to Reading Primers $R_0$ & $R_1$. Point to a sign <u>a</u> and ask your student: "How would you say this one?"
- Continue pointing (without speaking), giving your student the opportunity to say the sound and to listen to themself saying it. Spend only a few minutes on this, just the time required for your student to be sure which sound is associated with the sign <u>a</u>.
- Point to the other "words" on page 6 of Reading Primers $R_0$ & $R_1$ groups like <u>aa</u>, <u>aaa</u>, and listen to your student read them. If a difficulty arises, point back to a single <u>a</u> and ask: "What did you say for this one?" Then, "How many of these do you see in this group?" For example <u>aa</u>, "Say them as fast as possible," because they are close together.

# Table 0.1 Activity 1

## Teaching Techniques and Games

*Visual Dictation*

- Teacher uses the pointer: In Reading Primers $R_0$ & $R_1$, or on Chart 0 point to a single <u>a</u> a few times, varying both the number of taps and the rhythm. If for instance you touch <u>a</u> once, pause, and then touch it three times in rapid succession. Your student is likely to say: <u>a</u> (pause) <u>aaa</u>.
- Student uses the pointer: Your student points to a single <u>a</u> a few times, varying both the number of taps and the rhythm and you would produce the sounds to match.

*Oral Dictation*

- Student uses the pointer: Teacher would say the "words," and your student would then tap the signs with the same rhythm. For example: if the teacher says <u>a</u> <u>aa</u>, or <u>a</u> <u>aaa</u>, or <u>aa</u> <u>a</u> then your student would tap the corresponding sounds.

*Words in Color Toolbox*

- Look in the Words in Color Toolbox on page 83 for suitable games. Try:
  - Pre-Reading Rhythm Game, page 111
  - Pre-Reading Listening Game, page 112

# Table 0.2 Activity 1

### Sound / Spelling
- u as in up

### Materials
- Chart 0
- Reading Primers $R_0$ & $R_1$
- Pointer
- Fidel

### Beginning Notes

When you see au remember that it doesn't sound as in the word auto. The a and u are distinct sounds: the a sound as in pat and u as in up.

# Table 0.2 Activity 1

## Steps

- Using your pointer, point to <u>u</u> on Chart 0 and say its sound once. Remember you are not naming the alphabet, you are using the sound <u>u</u> as in <u>up</u>.

- Point to another <u>u</u> and ask your student to say the sound.

- Point to each sign in "<u>uu</u>" and ask your student to say the sounds. If they cannot say these sounds then say it once and ask them to say it.

- Point to each sign in "<u>uuu</u>" and ask your student to say the sounds. If they cannot say these sounds then say it once and ask them to say it.

- Switch to Table 0.2 in Reading Primers $R_0$ & $R_1$. Point to a sign <u>u</u> and ask your student: "How would you say this one?"

- Continue pointing (without speaking), giving your student the opportunity to say the sound and to listen to themselves saying it.

- Point to the other "words" on page 9 or 10 of Reading Primers $R_0$ & $R_1$ (groups like <u>au</u>, <u>uaa</u>), and listen to your student read them; if a difficulty arises, point back to a single <u>u</u> and ask: "What did you say for this one?" then, "How many of these do you see in this group?"

# Table 0.2 Activity 1

## Teaching Techniques and Games

*Point, Show, Engage 1*

- Using the single signs a and u tap in rhythm (for example, aa u) and ask your student:
    - "What did I show?"
    - "What would the reverse of this be?" or "How would you say it backwards?"
    - "Tap it yourself on the Fidel."

*Point, Show, Engage 2*

- Point to one of the "words" on page 9 or 10 of Reading Primers $R_0$ & $R_1$ and ask your student to read it. Then ask:
    - "What would the reverse of this be?" or "How do you say it backwards?"
    - "Is that (the reverse) written on this page?" Yes? No?
    - If yes, "Can you find it and show it to me?"

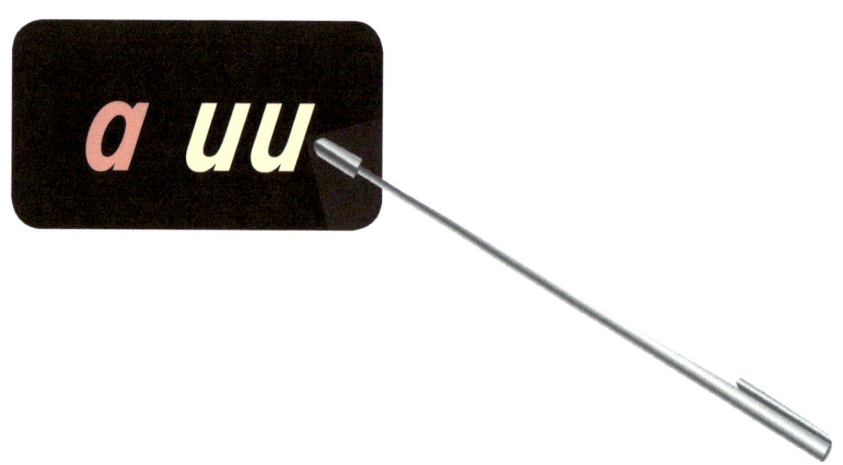

# Table 0.3, 0.4, 0.5 Activity 1

### Sound / Spelling
- i as in it
- e as in pet
- o as in pot

### Materials
- Chart 0
- Reading Primers $R_0$ & $R_1$
- Pointer
- Fidel

## Beginning Notes

We will now introduce the other three tables in $R_0$. It is a good idea to introduce each sound one at a time.

# Table 0.3, 0.4, 0.5 Activity 1

## Steps

- Repeat the process used for <u>a</u> and <u>u</u> and apply it to:
  - <u>i</u>   as in   <u>i</u>t
  - <u>e</u>   as in   p<u>e</u>t
  - <u>o</u>   as in   p<u>o</u>t

- At some point, your student may want to start writing the signs (letters) they know. At this point, <u>*do not worry about legibility or neatness.*</u> Let them write and read back to you what they have written.

- At the top of the Fidel Phonic Chart, show your student the location of the 5 signs with their respective colors (top left of the Fidel). Listed with them are all the other spellings that represent these sounds in English. You do not need at this stage to tell them why there are so many. But if you must, let them repeat the same sound every time you touch any other sign in the same column (and with the same color).

# Table 0.3, 0.4, 0.5 Activity 1

## Teaching Techniques and Games

*Oral Dictation*

Teacher says a "word" (<u>aiio</u>) or a "sentence" (<u>aai</u> <u>uu</u> <u>oei</u>) and your student then:

- Option 1: Finds the word and points to it.
- Option 2: Taps out the word or sentence.
- Option 3: Writes the word or sentence.

*Visual Dictation*

Teacher taps out a "word," for example <u>eeoa</u> or a "sentence" for example, <u>ea</u> <u>iea</u> <u>aoie</u>.

- Student says the word or sentence, then
- Student writes the word or sentence.
- Teacher asks, "What would the reverse of this be?"
- Teacher asks, "Tap it yourself on the Fidel."

*Words in Color Toolbox*

Look in the Words in Color Toolbox on page 83 for beginner games.

# Congratulations!

You have completed Reading Primer $R_0$ and introduced 5 basic vowel sounds.

You have also learned a few games and techniques that you can use throughout Words in Color. Before you progress to $R_1$, it is suggested you not progress further until your student feels comfortable in combining the various sounds and spellings introduced.

Take as much time as you like to practice and play around with the games and techniques we have presented.

For more tips please visit the Words in Color section at www.EducationalSolutions.com.

# $R_1$
# The Second Group of Activities

# Overview of $R_1$ Part 1

At the beginning of $R_1$ (see page 27 of the Reading Primers $R_0$ & $R_1$) you will find Word Building Table 1.

Word Building Table 1

This table is made of the five vowels studied in $R_0$ and introduces four new consonant sounds, with eight different spellings in all.

- The p and pp consonant, pronounced as in the words pat and puppet
- The t and tt consonant, pronounced as in the words tap and attempt
- The s consonant, pronounced as in the words is
- The s, ss, and 's consonants, pronounced as in the words us, pass, or it's

# Table 1.1 Activity 1

### Sound / Spelling
- Existing sounds/spellings:
  a  u  i  e  o
- New sound/spelling:
  p as in pat

### Materials
- Reading Primers $R_0$ & $R_1$
- Pointer
- Fidel

## Beginning Notes

- In English, consonants are never spoken in isolation; they are always combined with other sounds – the vowels. Take special care to always combine consonants with vowels to make syllables that can be spoken.

  - For example, we can't say p alone, because alone it is just air passing through our lips. Instead we always combine it with a vowel sound – pa, pu, etc. Since you can not pronounce a consonant in isolation, always combine it with a vowel sound, and pronounce it as a single sound – not as "puh-a," but as pa. Vowels placed next to each other are still pronounced separately.

- As you will be using the Fidel more in the following sections, we suggest you familiarize yourself with the Fidel Phonic Code. You can refer to Activity 2 on page 13 to help you locate sounds and words on the Fidel and Word Charts.

# Table 1.1 Activity 1

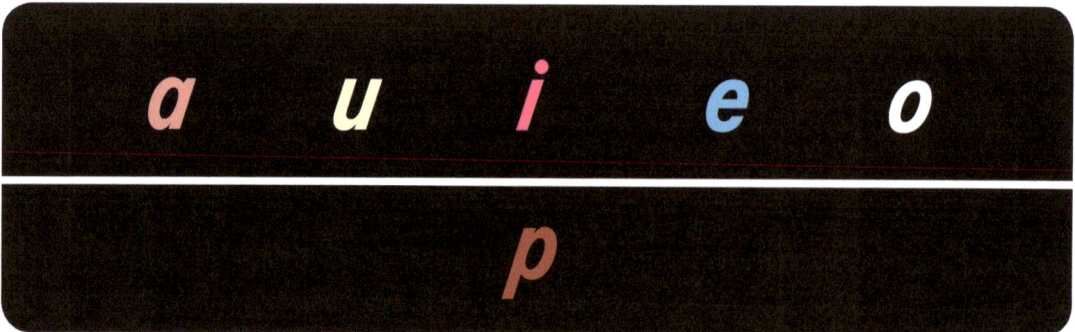

Table 1.1 from Reading Primers R₀ & R₁, page 28

## Steps

*Making Simple Syllables*

- In Table 1.1 of R₁, point to a vowel (for example, <u>a</u>) and ask your student to say it.
- Then sliding your pointer quickly from <u>a</u> to <u>p</u> say: "<u>a</u> followed by this one (<u>p</u>) is called <u>ap</u>."
- Say it only once then point again and let your student say it.
- At this time, it is not helpful and could be distracting to say "<u>ap</u> as in <u>app</u>le."
- Then slide your pointer from each of the other vowels to the <u>p</u> and let your student find out what to say for the resulting syllables. Ask them: "What would you say for this one?"

    - <u>u</u>    followed by  <u>p</u>  »  <u>up</u>
    - <u>i</u>    followed by  <u>p</u>  »  <u>ip</u>
    - <u>e</u>    followed by  <u>p</u>  »  <u>ep</u>
    - <u>o</u>    followed by  <u>p</u>  »  <u>op</u>

- Remember do not name the letters. At this time, just point to the vowel followed by the consonant.

# Table 1.1 Activity 1

## Teaching Techniques and Games

*Oral Dictation*

Teacher writes down, in large size, a number of syllables and "sentences" and says a syllable (<u>ap</u>) or a "sentence" (<u>ap up up op</u>) and your student then:

- Option 1: Finds the syllable or sentence and points to it on the paper.
- Option 2: Taps out the syllable or sentence on the Fidel or $R_1$.
- Option 3: Writes the syllable or sentence.

*Visual Dictation*

Teacher taps out a "syllable" for example, <u>ep</u> or a "sentence" for example, <u>ip apap ep</u>.

- Student says the syllable or "sentence," then
- Student writes the syllable or "sentence."
- Teacher asks, "What would the reverse of this be?"
- Teacher asks, "Tap it yourself."

# Table 1.1 Activity 2

### Sound / Spelling
- p as in pat

### Materials
- Chart 1
- Reading Primers $R_0$ & $R_1$
- Pointer

### Beginning Notes

_____
_____
_____
_____
_____
_____
_____
_____
_____
_____
_____

# Table 1.1 Activity 2

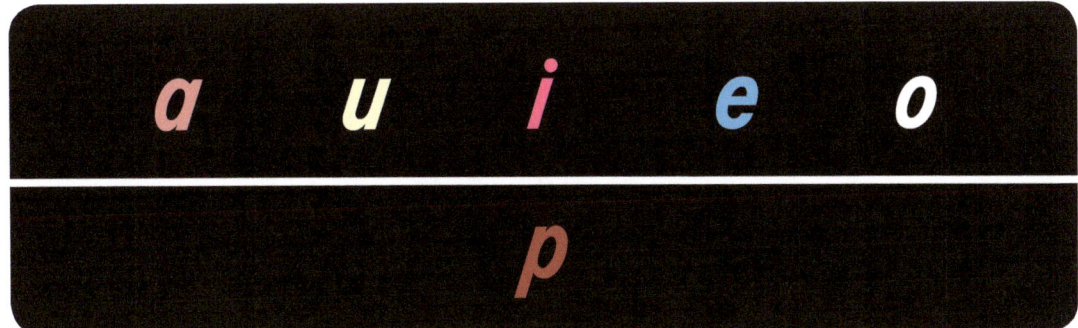

Table 1.1 from Reading Primers R₀ & R₁, page 28

## Steps

*Reversing Syllables*

- Using either Table 1.1 or the Fidel, slide your pointer from p to each of the other vowels and let your student find out what to say for the resulting syllables.

- Ask them: "What would you say for this one?"
    - p    followed by    a    »    pa
    - p    followed by    u    »    pu
    - p    followed by    i    »    pi
    - p    followed by    e    »    pe
    - p    followed by    o    »    po

- Make sure you give your student enough time to figure out how to sound out the syllables by themself.

- If you are having difficulties, go back to Table 1.1 Activity 1 on page 30.

# Table 1.1 Activity 2

## Teaching Techniques and Games

*Oral Dictation*

Teacher writes down, in large size, a number of syllables and "sentences" and says a syllable for example, pa or a "sentence" for example, pa pu pi pe and your student then:

- Option 1: Finds the syllable or sentence and points to it.
- Option 2: Taps out the syllable or sentence.
- Option 3: Writes the syllable or sentence.

*Visual Dictation*

Teacher taps out a syllable for example, pe or a "sentence" for example, pi pepapi pepu.

- Student says the syllable or "sentence," then
- Student writes the syllable or "sentence."
- Teacher asks, "What would the reverse of this be?"
- Teacher asks, "Tap it yourself."

*Words in Color Toolbox*

Look in the Words in Color Toolbox on page 83 for more games. If your student is having difficulty sounding out their first consonant, we recommend:

- Repeating the First Consonant, page 113
- Suzette's First Consonant Game, page 114
- First Consonant Game, page 116

# Table 1.1 Activity 3

**Sound / Spelling**
- p as in pat

**Materials**
- Chart 1
- Reading Primers $R_0$ & $R_1$
- Pointer

**Beginning Notes**

_____
_____
_____
_____
_____
_____
_____
_____
_____
_____

# Table 1.1 Activity 3

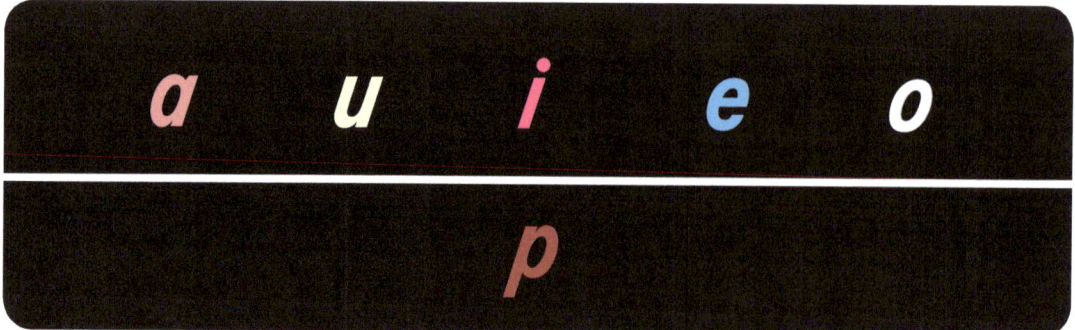

Table 1.1 from Reading Primers R₀ & R₁, page 28

## Steps

*Combining Syllables to Form Simple Words*

- Slide your pointer from the p to the a and then back to the p so that you have tapped out the "word" pap. Then let your student find out how you would pronounce this.

- Go slow and give a lot of time if needed. If they struggle with this, have them say pa and then ap to see if they can make the connection. If they continue to struggle, it is suggested you try the teaching technique "For Awareness of Blends," on page 95.

- Ask them: "What would you say for this one?"
    - p    followed by   a   followed by   p   »   pap
    - p    followed by   u   followed by   p   »   pup
    - p    followed by   i   followed by   p   »   pip
    - p    followed by   e   followed by   p   »   pep
    - p    followed by   o   followed by   p   »   pop

- Make sure you give your student enough time to figure out how to sound out the syllables by themself.

# Table 1.1 Activity 3

## Teaching Techniques and Games

*Oral Dictation*

- Teacher writes down, in large size, a number of words and "sentences" and says a word:
  - Option 1: Student finds the word points to it.
  - Option 2: Student taps out the word.
  - Option 3: Student writes the word.

*Visual Dictation*

- Teacher taps out a word
- Student says the syllable or "sentence," then
- Student writes the syllable or "sentence."
- Teacher asks, "What would the reverse of this be?"
- Teacher asks, "Tap it yourself."

*Substitution Game*

- Teacher writes a word, pop, and asks the student to read it. Then they write a second word, pap, and asks the student read it. Next the teacher asks the student which letter do I have to change if I want to transform the pop into the word pap. Continue this game with other words:
  - pip » pep
  - pep » pap
  - pep » pup
  - pop » pep
  - pip » pop, etc.

# Table 1.1 Activity 4

**Sound / Spelling**
- p as in pat

**Materials**
- Reading Primers $R_0$ & $R_1$
- Pointer
- Fidel

## Beginning Notes

Make sure you give your student enough time to figure out how to sound out the sentence by themselves. It is very important to give as much time as needed and not give the answers when your student encounters some difficulty. If it is too challenging, go back to the previous step and build up from there. All the achievements gained here will result in acceleration in subsequent studies if you do not give answers and give the time needed to figure out what is required.

# Table 1.1 Activity 4

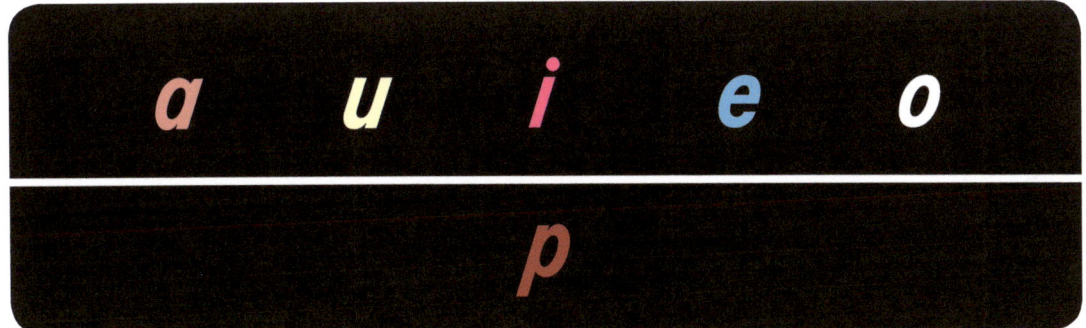

Table 1.1 from Reading Primers R₀ & R₁, page 28

## Steps

*Combining Syllables to Form Simple Sentences*

- You are now going to use your pointer and either Table 1.1 or the Fidel to tap out the simple sentence: pop up.
- First, tap the sequence p o p.
- Next you will need to indicate the space or pause between the word pop and up. To do this, use the pointer to tap in a neutral location, such as off the page or on the desk.
- Then tap the sequence u p.
- You will need to explain to your student that when you tap in the neutral location it indicates a new word. Practice this a few times until it is well understood. Then, tap out the following sentences and ask your student: "What would you say for..."

  - pop up
  - pep up
  - up up up
  - up pop up
  - pep up pop

# Table 1.1 Activity 4

## Teaching Techniques and Games

*Oral Dictation Game*

Extend the game you learned in Table 1.1 Activity 3 by:

- Tapping out a word or sentence and after it has been successfully spoken, tap it out again and add on to it. The game continues as long as each sequence is spoken correctly.
- Tapping out a word or sentence and saying it first in the usual way and then saying it in unusual ways by putting stress – loud or soft – on various parts of the sequence.

*Visual Dictation Game*

Extend the game you learned in Table 1.1 Activity 3 by saying sentences with different tones and expression:

- like you are asking a question
- like you are angry
- like you are happy
- like you are confused
- create your own unique ways of expression

*Substitution Game*

- "What word do you have to change to transform the first sentence into the second?  pop up  »  pep up."
- Continue this game and create your own sentences.


*Reversing Game*

- "What does a word like pip become when reversed?"
- "What does a sentence like up pop become when reversed?"  (Answer is "pop up")
- Continue this game with your own words and sentences.


*Words in Color Toolbox*

Look in the Words in Color Toolbox on page 83 for more games.

# Table 1.2 Activity 1

**Sound / Spelling**
- t as in test

**Materials**
- Reading Primers $R_0$ & $R_1$
- Pointer
- Fidel

## Beginning Notes

Make sure you give your student enough time to figure out how to sound out the sentence by himself or herself.

It is very important to give as much time as is needed and not to give the answers when your student encounters some difficulty. If it is too challenging, go back to the previous step and build up from there. All the achievements gained here will result in acceleration in subsequent studies if you do not give answers and give the time needed to figure out what is required.

Table 1.2 has a similar structure to Table 1.1. We are introducing the spelling t.

# Table 1.2 Activity 1

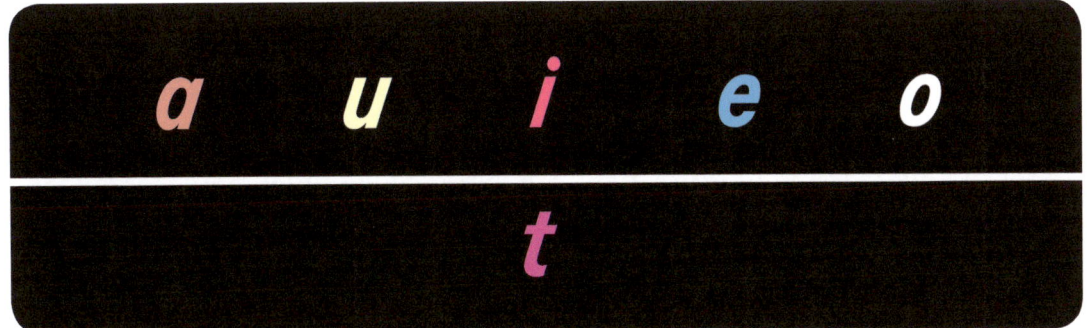

Table 1.2 from Reading Primers R₀ & R₁, page 30

## Steps

*Making Simple Syllables*

- Using Table 1.1 or the Fidel point to a vowel (for example, <u>a</u>) and ask your student to say it.

- Then sliding your pointer quickly from <u>a</u> to <u>t</u> say: "<u>a</u> followed by this one (<u>t</u>) is called <u>at</u>."

- Say it only once then point again and let your student say it.

- Then slide your pointer from each of the other vowels to the <u>t</u> and let your student find out what to say for the resulting syllables.  Ask them:  "What would you say for this one?"
    - <u>u</u>   followed by   <u>t</u>   »   <u>ut</u>
    - <u>i</u>   followed by   <u>t</u>   »   <u>it</u>
    - <u>e</u>   followed by   <u>t</u>   »   <u>et</u>
    - <u>o</u>   followed by   <u>t</u>   »   <u>ot</u>

- Remember do not name the letters.  At this time, just point to the vowel followed by the consonant.

# Table 1.2 Activity 1

## Teaching Techniques and Games

*Oral Dictation*

Teacher writes down, in large size, a number of syllables and "sentences" and says a syllable for example, <u>at</u> or a "sentence" for example, <u>at</u> <u>ut</u> <u>ut</u> <u>ot</u> and your student then:

- Option 1: Finds the syllable or sentence and points to it.
- Option 2: Taps out the syllable or sentence.
- Option 3: Writes the syllable or sentence.

*Visual Dictation*

Teacher taps out a "syllable" for example <u>et</u> or a "sentence" for example, <u>it</u> <u>at</u> <u>et</u>.

- Student says the syllable or "sentence," then
- Student writes the syllable or "sentence."
- Teacher asks, "What would the reverse of this be?"
- Teacher asks, "Tap it yourself."

*Words in Color Toolbox*

Look in the Words in Color Toolbox on page 83 for more games.

# Table 1.2 Activity 2

### Sound / Spelling
- <u>t</u> as in <u>t</u>es<u>t</u>

### Materials
- Reading Primers $R_0$ & $R_1$
- Pointer
- Fidel

### Beginning Notes

# Table 1.2 Activity 2

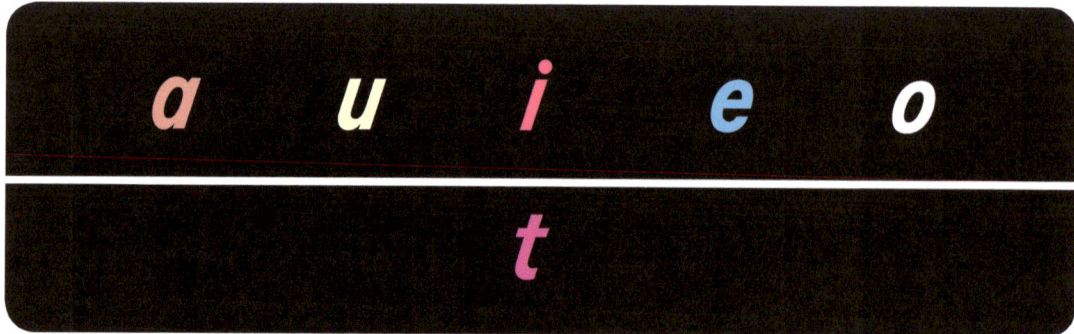

Table 1.2 from Reading Primers $R_0$ & $R_1$, page 30

## Steps

*Reversing Syllables*

- Using Table 1.2 or the Fidel, slide your pointer from <u>t</u> to each of the other vowels and let your student find out what to say for the resulting syllables.

- Ask them: "What would you say for this one?"
    - <u>t</u>    followed by  <u>a</u>  »  <u>ta</u>
    - <u>t</u>    followed by  <u>u</u>  »  <u>tu</u>
    - <u>t</u>    followed by  <u>i</u>  »  <u>ti</u>
    - <u>t</u>    followed by  <u>e</u>  »  <u>te</u>
    - <u>t</u>    followed by  <u>o</u>  »  <u>to</u>

- Make sure you give your student enough time to figure out how to sound out the syllables by themself.

# Table 1.2 Activity 2

## Teaching Techniques and Games

*Oral Dictation*

Teacher writes down, in large size, a number of syllables and "sentences" and says a syllable for example, <u>ta</u> or a "sentence" for example, <u>ta</u> <u>tu</u> <u>ti</u> <u>te</u> and your student then:

- Option 1: Finds the syllable or sentence and points to it.
- Option 2: Taps out the syllable or sentence.
- Option 3: Writes the syllable or sentence.

*Visual Dictation*

Teacher taps out a "syllable" for example, <u>te</u> or a "sentence" for example, <u>ti</u> <u>tetati</u> <u>tetu</u>.

- Student says the syllable or "sentence," then
- Student writes the syllable or "sentence."
- Teacher asks, "What would the reverse of this be?"
- Teacher asks, "Tap it yourself."

*Words in Color Toolbox*

Look in the Words in Color Toolbox on page 83 for more games.

# Table 1.2 Activity 3

**Sound / Spelling**
- t as in test

**Materials**
- Reading Primers $R_0$ & $R_1$
- Pointer
- Fidel

## Beginning Notes

_____
_____
_____
_____
_____
_____
_____
_____
_____
_____

# Table 1.2 Activity 3

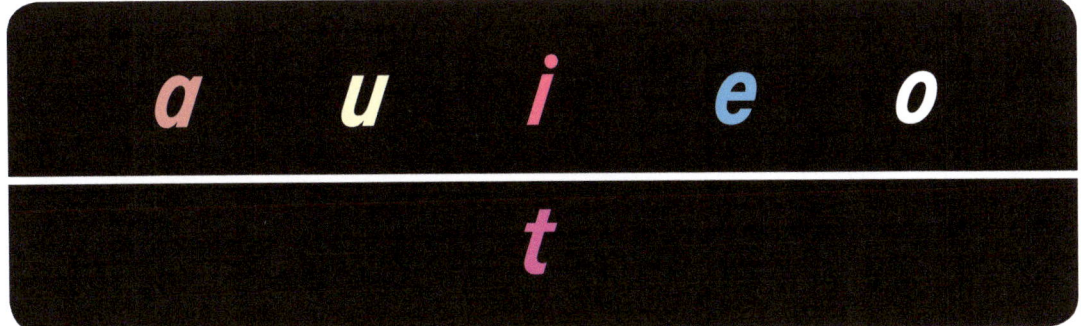

Table 1.2 from Reading Primers R₀ & R₁, page 30

## Steps

*Combining Syllables to Form Simple Words*

- Using Table 1.2 or the Fidel, slide your pointer from the t to the a and then back to the t so that you have tapped out the "word" tat. Then let your student find out how you would pronounce this. Go slow and give a lot of time if needed. If they struggle with this have them say ta and then at to see if they can make the connection.

- Ask them: "What would you say for this one?"

    - t         followed by     a       followed by     t       »       tat
    - t         followed by     u       followed by     t       »       tut
    - t         followed by     i       followed by     t       »       tit
    - t         followed by     e       followed by     t       »       tet
    - t         followed by     o       followed by     t       »       tot

- Make sure you give you student enough time to figure out how to sound out the syllables by themselves.

# Table 1.2 Activity 3

## Teaching Techniques and Games

*Oral Dictation*

- Teacher writes down, in large size, a number of words and "sentences" and says a word:
  - Option 1: Student finds the word points to it.
  - Option 2: Student taps out the word.
  - Option 3: Student writes the word.

*Visual Dictation*

- Teacher taps out a word,
- Student says the syllable or "sentence," then
- Student writes the syllable or "sentence."
- Teacher asks, "What would the reverse of this be?"
- Teacher asks, "Tap it yourself."

*Substitution Game*

- Teacher writes a word; tot and asks the student to read it. Then they write a second word; tat and asks the student read it. Next the teacher asks the student which letter do I have to change if I want to transform the tot into the word tat. Continue this game with other words:
  - tit » tet
  - tet » tat
  - tet » tut
  - tot » tet
  - tit » tot, etc.

# Table 1.2 Activity 4

**Sound / Spelling**
- t as in test

**Materials**
- Chart 1
- Reading Primers $R_0$ & $R_1$
- Pointer
- Fidel

## Beginning Notes

Make sure you give your student enough time to figure out how to sound out the sentence by themselves. It is very important to give as much time as needed and not give the answers when your student encounters some difficulty. If it is too challenging, go back to the previous step and build up from there. All the achievements gained here will result in acceleration in subsequent studies if you do not give answers and give the time needed to figure out what is required.

# Table 1.2 Activity 4

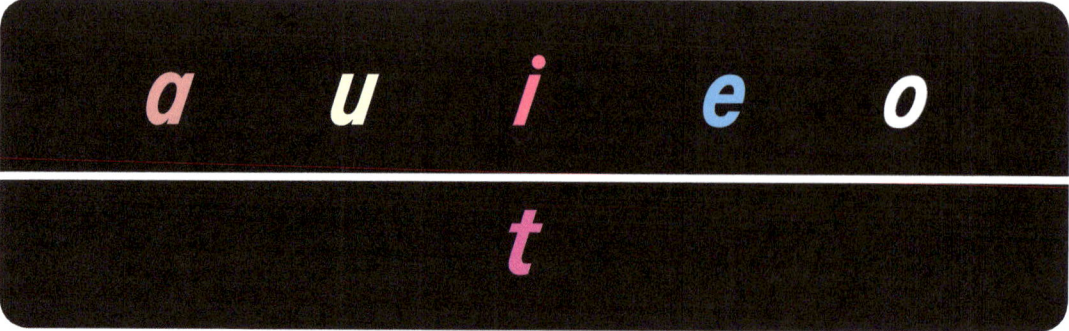

Table 1.2 from Reading Primers R₀ & R₁, page 30

## Steps

*Combining Words to Form Simple Sentences*

- Using Table 1.2 or the Fidel, you are now going to use your pointer to tap out the simple sentence: <u>at</u> <u>it</u>.

- First, tap the sequence <u>a</u> <u>t</u>.

- Next you will need to indicate the space or pause between the word at and it. To do this, use the pointer to tap in a neutral location, such as off the bottom of the page.

- Then tap the sequence <u>i</u> <u>t</u>.

- Then, tap out the following sentences and ask your student: "What would you say for…"
  - <u>at</u> <u>it</u>
  - <u>tot</u> <u>it</u> <u>up</u>
  - <u>tit</u> <u>tat</u>
  - <u>tat</u> <u>it</u>
  - <u>tut</u> <u>tut</u> <u>tut</u>

# Table 1.2 Activity 4

## Teaching Techniques and Games

*Oral Dictation Game*

Extend this game by:

- tapping out a word or sentence and after it has been successfully spoken, tap it out again and add on to it. The game continues as long as each sequence is spoken correctly.
- tapping out a word or sentence and saying it first in the usual way and then saying it in unusual ways by putting stress – loud or soft – on various parts of the sequence.

*Visual Dictation Game*

Extend this game by saying sentences in with different tones and expression:

- like you are asking a question
- like you are angry
- like you are happy
- like you are confused
- like you are singing
- create your own unique ways of expression

*Words in Color Toolbox*

Look in the Words in Color Toolbox on page 83 for more games.

Continued . . .

## Teaching Techniques and Games Continued...

*Reversing Game*

- "What does a word like tat become when reversed?"
- "What does a sentence like tit tat become when reversed?" (Answer is: tat tit)
- Continue this game with your own words and sentences.

*Practice Using Chart 1*

- Now that we have covered p and t, play the Oral Dictation Game using Chart 1: pat, pit, pet, pot, pop, at, it, up, tot, top, tip, tap, apt.
- At this point, we have left out putt, we will discuss this in Table 1.3.

# Table 1.3 Activity 1

### Sound / Spelling
- pp as in puppet
- tt as in putt

### Materials
- Chart 1
- Reading Primers $R_0$ & $R_1$
- Pointer
- Fidel

## Beginning Notes

In this Table, we introduce our first ambiguity. We will show that a different spelling can have a similar sound. We will introduce the student to the spelling pp and tt.

Notice that the pp and tt are located in the same column as p and t on the Fidel. This indicates they have the same sound. Ask the student "What do you notice about the spellings pp and tt?" They might say that they have the same color or they are in the same column as the signs p and t respectively.

Make sure you give your student enough time to figure out how to sound out the sentence by himself or herself. It is very important to give as much time as needed and not give the answers when your student encounters some difficulty. If it is too challenging, go back to the previous step and build up from there. All the achievements gained here will result in acceleration in subsequent studies if you do not give answers and give the time needed to figure out what is required.

# Table 1.3 Activity 1

Table 1.3 from Reading Primers R₀ & R₁, page 32

## Steps

Note: Depending on the pace of your student, you may break the steps below into multiple lessons.

*Making Simple Syllables and Forming Simple Words*

Tap out various spellings (using Table 1.3 or the Fidel) and ask the student to say the words.

- p      followed by u      followed by tt      »      putt
- p      followed by i      followed by tt      »      pitt
- p      followed by o      followed by tt      »      pott
- t      followed by o      followed by pp      »      topp

Break the above into 3 steps if the student is having trouble. i.e. p followed by u; then u followed by tt; then combine to form putt.

*Combining Words to Form Simple Sentences*

Use the techniques described in Activities for previous Tables to form the sentences found in the section under Table 1.3 in $R_1$:

- tap it
- pitt tip it up
- tip it up pitt
- putt it, etc.

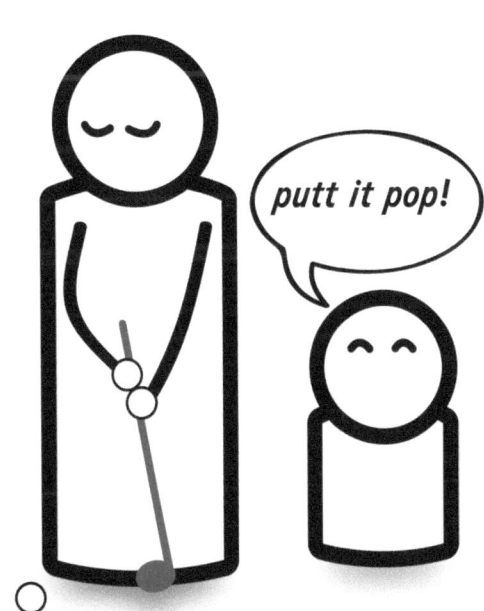

# Table 1.3 Activity 1

## Teaching Techniques and Games

At this stage, you should be familiar with the games and exercises we have introduced in the previous lessons. We have summarized them in the Words in Color Toolbox found on page 83. It is suggested you incorporate some of the following techniques to add variety, and increase interest for your student:

- Oral Dictation
- Visual Dictation
- Substitution Game
- Reversing Game
- Suitable games from the Words in Color Toolbox on page 83.

Practice these games using Chart 1. Add the word <u>putt</u> found on the second line in Chart 1 to the game played in Table 1.2 Activity 4. Tap out different sentences using Chart 1 by building on the knowledge gained in previous lessons.

# Table 1.4 Activity 1

| Sound / Spelling | Materials |
|---|---|
| • s as in is | • Chart 1<br>• Reading Primers $R_0$ & $R_1$<br>• Pointer<br>• Fidel |

## Beginning Notes

In this Table, we introduce another ambiguity with s. The letter s can have multiple sounds. For example, the letter s in the word is sounds differently than the word us. In this section, we are introducing the "lilac" s as in is. This is the 3rd column on the bottom half of the Fidel. Later, in Table 1.6, we will introduce the "lime green" s as in us.

Make sure you give your student enough time to figure out how to sound out the sentence by himself or herself. It is very important to give as much time as is needed and not to give the answers when your student encounters some difficulty. If it is too challenging, go back to the previous step and build up from there. All the achievements gained here will result in acceleration in subsequent studies if you do not give answers and give the time needed to figure out what is required.

# Table 1.4 Activity 1

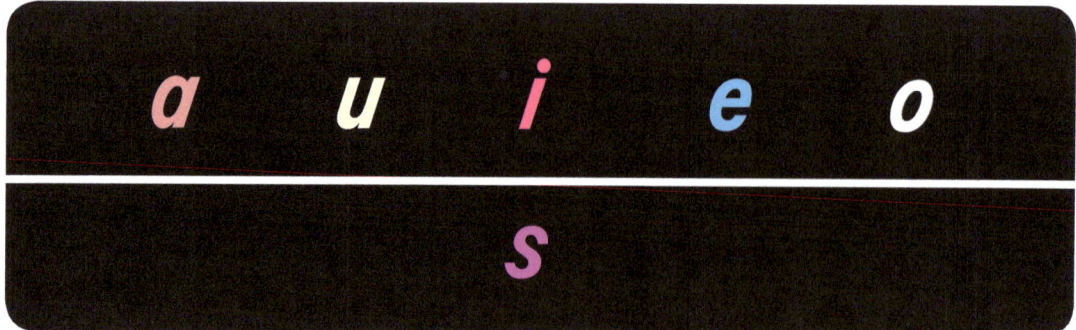

Table 1.4 from Reading Primers $R_0$ & $R_1$, page 36

## Steps

Note: Depending on the pace of your student, you may break the below into multiple lessons.

*Making Simple Syllables and Forming Simple Words*

- Tap out various spellings (using Table 1.4 or the Fidel) and ask the student to say the words.
    - a    followed by s    »    as
    - u    followed by s    »    us (remember to say it like uz)
    - i    followed by s    »    is
    - e    followed by s    »    es
    - o    followed by s    »    os

*Combining Words to Form Simple Sentences*

- Use the techniques described in Activities for previous Tables to form the sentences found in the section under Table 1.4 in $R_1$:
    - as is, etc.

# Table 1.4 Activity 1

## Teaching Techniques and Games

It is suggested you incorporate some of the following techniques to add variety, and increase interest for your student:

- Oral Dictation
- Visual Dictation
- Substitution Game
- Reversing Game
- Practice Using Chart 1
- Suitable games from the Words in Color Toolbox on page 83.

Add the words <u>as</u> and <u>is</u> found on the fourth line in Chart 1 to the game played in Table 1.2 Activity 4. Tap out different sentences using Chart 1 by building on the knowledge gained in previous lessons.

As a note, you may have noticed <u>-s</u> on Word Chart 1. This represents a plural form of the word. This will be discussed in Table 1.6.

# Table 1.5 Activity 1

> **Sound / Spelling**
> - No new sounds/spellings

> **Materials**
> - Chart 1
> - Reading Primers $R_0$ & $R_1$
> - Pointer
> - Fidel

## Beginning Notes

In this Table, we practice the spellings we have already covered to build more complex sentences.

# Table 1.5 Activity 1

Table 1.5 from Reading Primers $R_0$ & $R_1$, page 38

## Steps

- Depending on the pace of your student, you may break the below into multiple lessons.
  - Try making simple syllables and combining syllables to form simple words.
  - Try combining words to form simple sentences.

- Use the techniques described in Activities for previous Tables to form the sentences found in the section under Table 1.5 in $R_1$:
  - is it
  - is it pop
  - is pop up
  - pat is as apt as pitt is , etc.

# Table 1.5 Activity 1

## Teaching Techniques and Games

It is suggested you incorporate some of the following techniques to add variety, and increase interest for your student:

- Oral Dictation
- Visual Dictation
- Substitution Game
- Reversing Game
- Practice Using Chart 1
- Suitable games from the Words in Color Toolbox on page 83.

Tap out different sentences using Chart 1 by building on the knowledge gained in previous lessons.

As a note, you may have noticed -s on Word Chart 1. This represents a plural form of the word. This will be discussed in Table 1.6.

# Table 1.6 Activity 1

### Sound / Spelling
- <u>s</u> as in u<u>s</u>
- <u>'s</u> as in tom<u>'s</u>
- <u>ss</u> as in a<u>ss</u>et

### Materials
- Chart 1
- Reading Primers $R_0$ & $R_1$
- Pointer
- Fidel

### Beginning Notes

In this Table, we introduce another ambiguity with <u>s</u>. The letter <u>s</u> can have multiple sounds. For example, the letter <u>s</u> in the word i<u>s</u> sounds differently than the word u<u>s</u>. In this section, we are introducing the "lime green" <u>s</u> as in u<u>s</u>. This is the 4th column on the bottom half of the Fidel. Previously, in Table 1.4, we introduced the "lilac" <u>s</u> as in i<u>s</u>.

# Table 1.6 Activity 1

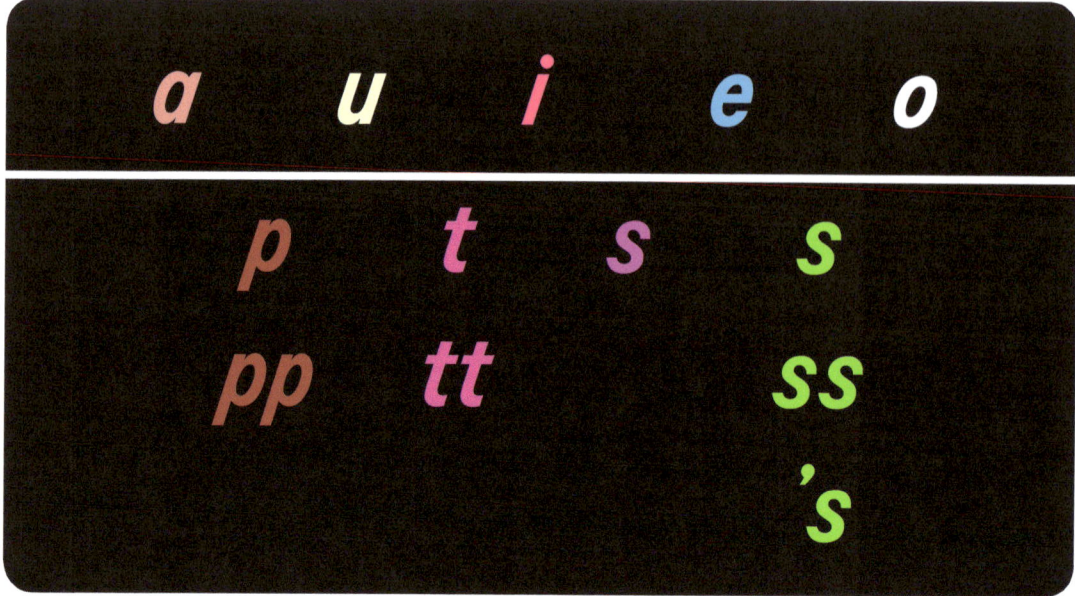

Table 1.6 from Reading Primers $R_0$ & $R_1$, page 40

## Steps

Note: Depending on the pace of your student, you may break the below into multiple lessons.

- Making simple syllables and forming simple words:
  - as
  - us     (here, pronounce it as you would the word us)
  - is     (here, pronounce it as you would the word this), etc.

- Introduce the possessive form of nouns and contractions:
  - Possessive: pat's, pitt's
  - Contractions: it's, it's pitt, it's pop
  - Combining words to form simple sentences: it's pat's pop.

- Use the techniques described in Activities for previous Tables to form the sentences found in the section under Table 1.6 in $R_1$.

# Table 1.6 Activity 1

## Teaching Techniques and Games

It is suggested you incorporate some of the following techniques to add variety, and increase interest for your student:

- Oral Dictation
- Visual Dictation
- Substitution Game
- Reversing Game
- Practice Using Chart 1
- Suitable games from the Words in Color Toolbox on page 83.

Tap out different sentences using Chart 1 by building on the knowledge gained in previous lessons.

We have not covered the letter e in the word puppet on Word Chart 1. As you may have noticed the color of e is the same as i, thus pronounced the same. Ask your student to try to pronounce this word. He or she may be able to get it immediately. Do not be tempted to give the answer, but instead provide leading questions such as:

- "What do you notice about this letter?"

If they are still stuck, you can ask them:

- "What color is the e? Does it look like any other color we have covered?"

# Overview of R₁ Part 2

On page 45 Reading Primers R₀ & R₁ you will find Word Building Table 2.

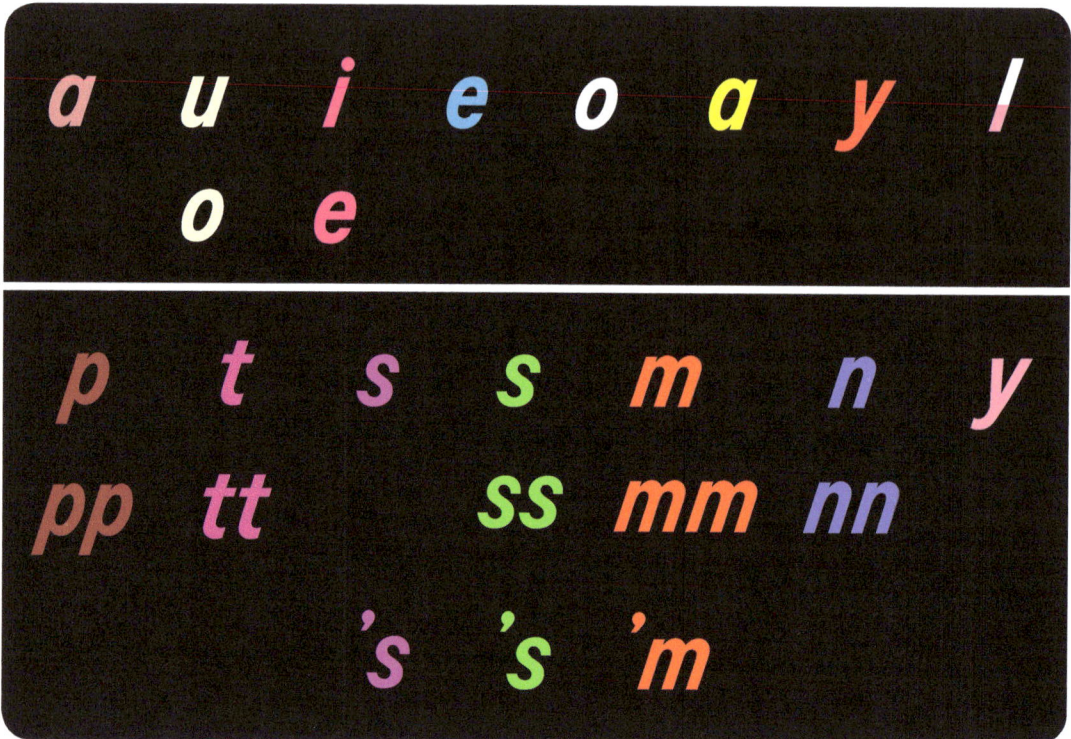

Word Building Table 2

This table is made of the five vowels studied in R₀ the four consonant sounds, with eight different spellings that were introduced in Tables 1.1-1.6 and adds:

The vowels:
- a as in the article a and assistant
- o as in son
- y as in puppy
- I as in the first person I

The consonants:
- <u>m</u> as in <u>m</u>an
- <u>mm</u> as in mo<u>mm</u>y
- <u>n</u> as in pa<u>n</u>t
- <u>nn</u> as in pe<u>nn</u>y
- <u>'m</u> as in I<u>'m</u>
- <u>y</u> as in <u>y</u>es

By the end of the next two Tables, you will have completed $R_1$. We suggest you practice using the same discipline as you did in previous sections to ensure the student clearly grasps the sound, spelling and concepts.

# Table 2.1 Activity 1

> **Sound / Spelling**
> - <u>m</u> as in <u>m</u>an
> - '<u>m</u> as in I'<u>m</u>
> - <u>a</u> as in the article <u>a</u>
> - <u>I</u> as in the first person <u>I</u>

> **Materials**
> - Chart 2
> - Reading Primers $R_0$ & $R_1$
> - Pointer
> - Fidel

## Beginning Notes

On Chart 2 there are two signs that some beginners tend to confuse and which we do not introduce by name, but by color: the "orange" three-legged <u>m</u> and the "lavender" two-legged <u>n</u>. Thus, we have broken these two spellings into two lessons.

There are more examples of words using the new sounds and spellings than there are in this guide. Consult the Reference Guide to the Fidel Phonic Code for more examples.

# Table 2.1 Activity 1

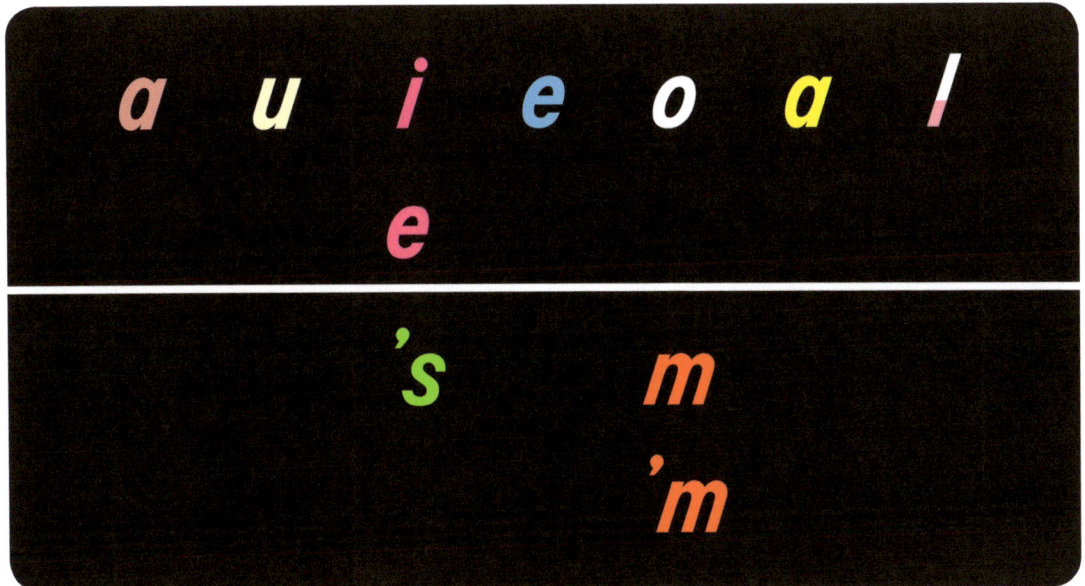

Table 2.1 from Reading Primers R₀ & R₁, page 46

## Steps

Note: Depending on the pace of your student, you may break the below into multiple lessons.

*Making Simple Syllables and Forming Simple Words*
- Tap out various spellings (using Table 2.1 or the Fidel) and ask the student to say the words.
    - <u>a</u>    followed by    <u>tt</u> <u>e</u> <u>m</u> <u>p</u> <u>t</u>    »    <u>attempt</u>
    - <u>m</u>    followed by    <u>a</u> <u>t</u>    »    <u>mat</u>
    - <u>p</u>    followed by    <u>u</u> <u>m</u> <u>p</u>    »    <u>pump</u>
    - etc.

Continued . . .

71

## Steps Continued...

*Combining Words to Form Simple Sentences*

• Use the techniques described in Activities for previous Tables to form the sentences found in the section under Table 2.1 in $R_1$:

- <u>it</u> <u>is</u> <u>mom's</u>
- <u>I</u> <u>miss</u> <u>pop</u>
- etc.

# Table 2.1 Activity 1

## Teaching Techniques and Games

It is suggested you incorporate some of the following techniques to add variety, and increase interest for your student:

- Oral Dictation
- Visual Dictation
- Substitution Game
- Reversing Game
- Suitable games from the Words in Color Toolbox on page 83.

*Practice Using Chart 2*

Use various games to practice Chart 2.
- Build upon previous knowledge to read the words on this chart. By this stage the student will be able to read words such as:
  - mat tim met tom mom must mumps mast I mops miss mess pump am stamps map sum I'm and pam

# Table 2.2 Activity 1

### Sound / Spelling
- <u>mm</u> as in mo<u>mm</u>y
- <u>n</u> as in pa<u>n</u>t
- <u>nn</u> as in pe<u>nn</u>y
- <u>y</u> as in <u>y</u>es
- <u>o</u> as in s<u>o</u>n
- <u>y</u> as in pupp<u>y</u>

### Materials
- Chart 2
- Reading Primers $R_0$ & $R_1$
- Pointer
- Fidel

## Beginning Notes

# Table 2.2 Activity 1

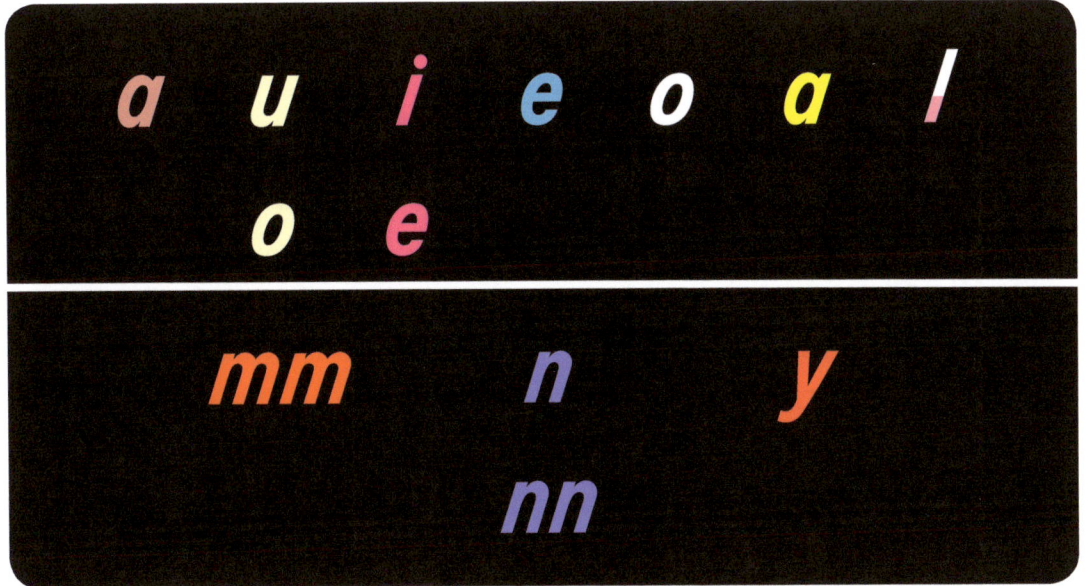

Table 2.2 from Reading Primers $R_0$ & $R_1$, page 50

## Steps

*Making Simple Syllables and Forming Simple Words*

- Tap out various spellings and ask the student to say the words.
    - <u>o</u>   followed by  <u>n</u>   »   <u>on</u>
    - <u>y</u>   followed by  <u>u</u> <u>mm</u> <u>y</u>   »   <u>yummy</u>

  (This example gives two sounds of the spelling <u>y</u>)
    - etc.

*Combining Words to Form Simple Sentences*

- Use the techniques described in Activities for previous Tables to form the sentences found in the section under Table 2.2 in $R_1$:
    - <u>sam</u> <u>is</u> <u>a</u> <u>man</u>
    - <u>I</u> <u>miss</u> <u>pop</u>
    - etc.

# Table 2.2 Activity 1

## Teaching Techniques and Games

It is suggested you to incorporate some of the following techniques to add variety, and increase interest for your student:
- Oral Dictation
- Visual Dictation
- Substitution Game
- Reversing Game
- Suitable games from the Words in Color Toolbox on page 83.
- Practice Using Chart 2

*Use Various Games to Practice Chart 2*
- Build upon previous knowledge to read the words on this chart. By this stage the student will be able to read words such as:
  - not nut net ten man men tent spent sent pants pin sun an in on son tempt attempt and assistant

*Practice Using Charts 1 & 2*

- Build on the challenge by constructing a sentence using words learned in both Charts 1 and 2.

*Practice Using the Fidel*

- For an even more challenging exercise, spell out the words in a sentence using the Fidel. Tap out each spelling separately to make a sentence such as:
  - p a t (blank) i s (blank) a (blank) m a n
  - The student should then say: pat is a man

# Congratulations!

You have completed Reading Primers $R_0$ & $R_1$ and introduced several vowel and consonant sounds.

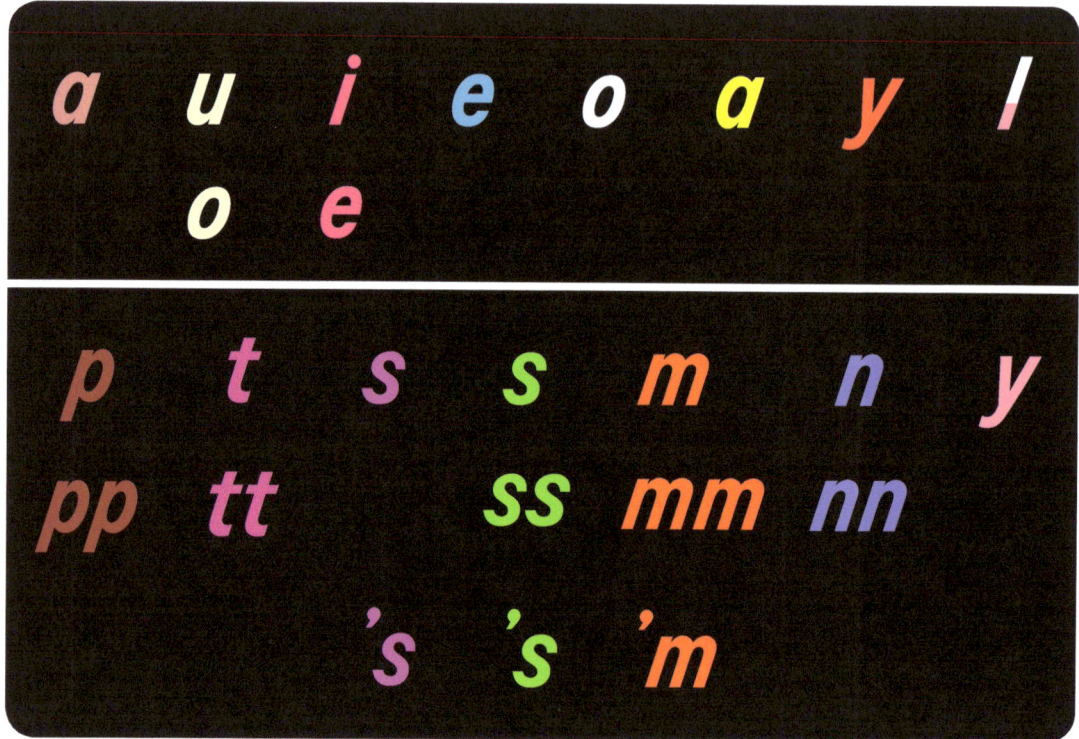

Word Building Table 2 from Reading Primers $R_0$ & $R_1$, page 45

Your student can now begin working on Worksheet 1 found in Workbook 1. If your student is able to pass through the exercises with ease, they can move on to Worksheet 2.

If they are having difficulties with it, it may be beneficial to review some of the previous lessons. By having a solid footing in the concepts introduced above, your student will be able to more easily master the work ahead.

Before you progress to $R_2$, it is suggested that the student feel comfortable in combining the various sounds and spellings introduced.

# $R_2$, $R_3$ and Beyond

# Overview of $R_2$, $R_3$ and Beyond

Now that we have shown you the basics to getting started and introduced basic words and sentences, you are now ready to progress to $R_2$.

Moving forward, we suggest you introduce each sound one at a time using the following techniques:

- Find the sound on the Fidel. If you are having difficulty finding it on the Fidel, use the Color Key for the American English Fidel.

- Tap out the new sound. Remember, you can introduce vowel sounds in isolation, but you must introduce consonants with vowels. For example, to introduce f as in if, tap out i then f for example.

- Next, play around with the new sound by combining it with sounds the student already knows. For example, f with a as in at, f with a as in was, etc. At this point it is not important for the words to be real English words as long as the student is correctly identifying the spelling with the correct sound.

- Practice by finding words on the Word Charts that include the new spelling.

- Then, practice by reading the words and sentences in the student's Reading Primer books $R_0$ & $R_1$, $R_2$, $R_3$), then use the Worksheets in Workbooks 1 & 2.

For further resources on how to use and apply Words in Color, please visit the Words in Color section of www.EducationalSolutions.com or visit our blog at www.Re-inventEd.com.

# Words in Color Toolbox

*Teaching Techniques & Games*

# Table of Contents
## *Words in Color Toolbox*

Teaching Techniques ............................................................87

Games ......................................................................................109

# Words in Color Toolbox
## *TEACHING TECHNIQUES*

# Teaching Technique: Visual Dictation 1

This game is played with the Fidel, and a pointer:
- The teacher taps out a sequence of signs, for example: p a t
- When the teacher has finished tapping out the sequence the student says the word: pat

The rhythm and speed of tapping can be varied to make the game more challenging and more interesting. The complexity and difficulty can be increased or decreased by varying the length of the sequences tapped. For example:

- p a » p a t » p a t s

Depth of understanding can be assessed by varying the sequence of signs tapped. For example:

- p a t s » p a s t » s p a t » s p a t s » t a p s

When a student has read the word successfully, the teacher may ask them:
- To tap the word on the Fidel themselves.
- To close their eyes and take a mental photograph of the whole word. This helps with retention.
- To close their eyes and tap the same sequence in the their mind – the teacher could ask them: Can you see the first sign, the second, the third and so on. This helps with retention.

## Continued . . .

# Continued: Visual Dictation 1

- To close their eyes, tap the sequence forward and say the word out loud, then ask what is the reverse of this – say the word, then tap it out. After they have done this with their eyes closed, the teacher could ask them to do it again on the charts. This helps with achieving high levels of performance and retention.
- Say the word with different tones of expression. For example: with happiness, with anger, with confusion, with skepticism, etc. This helps with understanding meaning.

The teacher may also ask one student to assume the role of teacher. In this scenario, one student taps out the sequence, another student reads aloud what has been tapped out.

The teacher could then ask another student, or the whole class; "What do you think? Is it correct?" If they feel it is not correct, the teacher could ask them tap the correct sequence themselves. There are several ways the question can be asked:

- "Is it correct?"
- "What do you think?"
- "Are you 100% sure?"
- "How would change it?"

# Teaching Techniques: Visual Dictation 2

Visual Dictation 2 has one difference from Visual Dictation 1 – it uses words from the word charts and not the Fidel. For example:

- Using word chart 1, the teacher would tap: <u>pat</u> <u>is</u> <u>top</u>.
- Following this, the student would read aloud the sequence of words tapped.
- If the student has difficulty with one word, the teacher can help them to work through it by using the Fidel and Visual Dictation 1.
- Once the student has worked through the difficult word, then the teacher would re-tap: <u>pat</u> <u>is</u> <u>top</u>.
- Following this, the student would read aloud the sequence of words.

All other techniques applicable for Visual Dictation 1 would apply to Visual Dictation 2.

# Teaching Technique: Oral Dictation 1

This game is played with the Fidel, and a pointer.
- The teacher says a word for example: <u>pat</u>
- The student would then tap out the sequence of signs corresponding to the word: <u>p</u> <u>a</u> <u>t</u>.

The rhythm and speed of the spoken word can be varied to make the game more challenging and more interesting. The complexity and difficulty can be increased or decreased by varying the length of the words or syllables spoken. For example

- <u>pa</u> » <u>pat</u> » <u>pats</u>

Depth of understanding can be assessed by using words that have very similar sounds, but small differences in spelling the sequence of signs tapped. For example, the teacher might say two words and then ask the student to tap them out on the Fidel:

- <u>pats</u> » <u>past</u>    or    <u>spat</u> » <u>spots</u>

Next the teacher might ask: "In what ways are these words different?"

When a student has tapped the word successfully, the teacher may ask them:
- To close their eyes and imagine tapping the word on the Fidel themselves. The teacher could ask them: "What's the first sign/color? The second? The third?" And so on. This helps with retention.
- To take a mental photograph of the word. This helps with retention.

Continued . . .

# Continued: Oral Dictation 1

To close their eyes, tap the sequence forward and say it out loud. Then ask: "What is the reverse of this?" "Say the word, then tap it out." After they have done this with their eyes closed, the teacher could ask them to do it again on the charts. This helps with achieving high levels of performance and retention.

- Which chart the word is on, and then ask them to find it.
- To say the word with different tones of expression. For example: with happiness, with anger, with confusion, with skepticism, etc. This helps with understanding meaning.

The teacher may also ask one student to assume the role of teacher. In this scenario, one student would say the word, another one then taps out the sequence, and yet another student reads aloud what has been tapped out.

The teacher could then ask another student, or the whole class; "What do you think? Is it correct?" If they feel it is not correct, the teacher could ask them tap the correct sequence themselves. There are several ways the question can be asked:

- "Is it correct?"
- "What do you think?"
- "Are you 100% sure?"
- "How would change it?"

# Teaching Technique: Oral Dictation 2

Oral Dictation 2 has one difference from Oral Dictation 1 – it incorporates words from the word charts in addition to the Fidel. For example:

- Using word chart 1, the teacher would say: <u>top</u> <u>it</u> <u>up</u>.
- Following this, the student would say a loud the sequence of words and then proceed to tap them out.
- If the student has difficulty with one word, the teacher can help then work through it by using the Fidel and Oral Dictation 1.
- When the student has worked through the difficult word, then the teacher would say the full sequence again: <u>top</u> <u>it</u> <u>up</u>.
- The student would then proceed to tap out the sequence again.
- All other techniques applicable for Oral Dictation 1 would apply to Oral Dictation 2.

# Teaching Technique: For Awareness of Blends

We have found that some beginning, or very young, readers struggle with word blends or combining syllables. For example, if you are trying to help your student go from the syllables pa and at to the word pat, the following technique may be helpful.

The teacher would tell students:

- "Take this sound pa and put it in this hand (the left hand) and make a fist."
- "Take this sound ap, put it in the other hand (right hand) and make a fist."
- "What do you have in this hand (the left one)?"
- "What do you have in the other one (the right one)?"
- "Say this one (the left one), now say the other one (the right one)."
- "Now let's take our hands and put them close together – say the sounds in each hand."
- "Now let's put our hands closer still – say the sounds."
- "Next let's put them right beside each other – say the sounds."
- "Now let's clap our hands together – how do we say the sound now?"

At this point some students may pause to think through how they would say the sound. It is important that you give them time to work it out. If they don't immediately get it or if they give up, it is suggested that you do not give the answer to them. Rather, try the exercise again. A second time through might trigger something which leads to an awareness of how to say the sound.

This technique can be used with other sounds, and in different orders. For example:

- pa and at » pat
- ta and ap » tap

# Teaching Technique: Reversing Game

The Reversing Game will help the student work through a mental exercise of trying to spell and read words and sentences that are in reverse order. For example, the teacher could write a word or sentence on the board, and then ask:

- "What does a word like pip become when reversed?" (Answer is pip)
- "What does a sentence like up pop become when reversed?" (Answer is pop up)

# Teaching Technique: The Gap Game

This game is played to develop insight into word formation. The teacher could start with an example of how to play the game by saying:

- "Lets look at the word pat."
- "If we replace p by a gap it will look like _ a t and many words can come to mind, like fat, sat, and mat."
- "If we replace a by a gap we get p _ t and other words come to mind like pit, pet, and pot."
- "If we replace t by a gap we get pa _ which brings to mind pass, pad, and pam."
- "Now lets play this game with the following words…"

As long as this game is interesting to all, you can play this game for hours just starting with any word already met and creating a gap for which perhaps there is more than one answer. Of course, only expect the gap to be filled by sounds already met. If they have not met m, don't introduce the examples pam or mat.

*The Gap Game Demonstrates:*

- That signs can be taken out of words, from any place, and the words can still be developed by the learners;
- That the student's image of words is flexible enough so that an incomplete pattern can bring about a number of answers;
- That the same word can provide answers to a number of differently formulated questions;
- That not all questions have the same number of answers. There is no obligation to start with the first column; any example can be a starting point.

# Teaching Technique: Reading Upside-Down

A good way to test decoding skills of the student is to have him or her read the words and sentences upside-down. This should only be done with words and sentences that they have already mastered since it will test their ability to know what is the correct orientation of the spellings and which direction to read.

A way to make this more fun is to time them while they attempt various sentences.

# Teaching Technique: Point, Show, Engage

This is typically used in the earlier stages for beginning readers to get them acquainted with the conventions of reading.

## Variation 1 Example:

Using the single signs a and u tap in rhythm (for example, aa u) and ask your student:

- "What did I show?"
- "What would the reverse of this be?"
- "Tap it yourself on the Fidel."

## Variation 2 Example:

Point to one of the "words" in the Primer books and ask your student to read it. Then ask:

- "What would the reverse of this be?"
- "Is it written on this page?" Yes? No?
- If yes, "Can you find it and show it to me?"

# Teaching Technique: For Awareness of Spelling

We can indicate the spelling of words by moving or tapping the pointer from sign to sign. This enables the student to understand that the order of the letters corresponds to how the words are spoken.

For example, if you want the student to say the word <u>pat</u>, you would tap the pointer on each letter in order on the Fidel or on the word chart:

<u>p</u> <u>a</u> <u>t</u>

For students who have come to think of spelling mainly as the individual letters, awareness of the sounds in words can be renewed during the more difficult levels of spelling. First point to the entire columns where the sounds are found. For the example <u>pat</u>, this is the whole chestnut column, the whole buff column, and the whole fuchsia column. Then during a second pointing, find the exact sign in each column required for correctly spelling a particular word.

Note: this technique is used in both Visual, and Oral Dictation for individual/small groups/classrooms.

### *If you are using Words in Color in a small group or larger classroom:*

- It is suggested that the person tapping stands to the side of the charts as to not obstruct the view of others.
- Allow other students to participate by asking individuals to go through the exercises.
- If students are imprecise with their pointing, the teacher can ask; "Can you be more exact? I am not clear what you are showing."
- In situations where the correct spelling is important, the teacher could say: "For the sake of spelling, lets use these…. signs."

# Teaching Technique: For Criteria and Autonomy

Ask a student, possibly the most advanced, to say each of the sounds as the teacher taps them out. (Oral Dictation)

The exercise can be reversed – i.e. the teacher says the sounds and one of the students points them out.

Then, ask the other students in the class to participate in determining whether the columns and the specific signs within the columns are being spoken or tapped correctly.

The doubts expressed by the students are examined and proper changes are made as required with regard to columns or signs within a column.

Instead of directly correcting them, students should be given opportunities to correct their own and one another's mistakes. Use probing questions or commands such as:

- "Are you sure you said it right?"
- "Are you 100% sure?"
- "Say it again."
- "Did he point it out correctly?"
- "Did she say it correctly?"
- "What is different between what was spoken and what was pointed out?"

This technique allows students to learn to choose correctly through the process of elimination and to take responsibility for their learning. It also allows students to take care of mistakes consciously, while working in a cooperative spirit.

# Teaching Technique: Active Visualization for Retention

In order to actively involve students' power of evocation, we suggest that students close their eyes and note if they can mentally develop a whole word which corresponds to the words they have shown on the Fidel, Word Charts or have seen somewhere else.

This technique generates self-reliance in students and prepares them to feel confident when they are right.

For example, after a student taps out a word, the teacher might say:
- "Close your eyes."
- "Can you see the word?"
- "If not open your eyes and take a look at it."
- "Now close your eyes again, can you picture it?"
- "It is clear? Do you have a strong picture?"
- "If not open your eyes and take a look again."
- "Lets try again, close your eyes and see it in detail."

In this way, difficult words, or pairs of words that have some similar attributes can be examined, and processed thoroughly.

# Teaching Technique: Writing

The next activity is to let students write down, on paper or on the chalkboard, the words they have formed on the Fidel and evoked in their minds.

It can be fun for students to exchange their notebooks, to read what others have written, and to discuss the correct way of writing words and showing them on the Fidel.

Since students meet the words again and again in the course of various learning activities — such as pointing out, evoking, writing down, and reading back — the drudgery of repetition is avoided.

These techniques also give continuous feedback, which allows teachers to evaluate all the time the learning taking place.

Soon after beginning to use the Fidel, teachers and students can make the observation that the signs given at the top of the columns occur in a number of words while less and less frequent spellings appear lower down in the columns. Presenting the whole of the Fidel gives students a sense of the way their language behaves, awakens their curiosity and maintains their interest in what they have yet to learn.

# Teaching Technique: Introducing a New Sound

The student may be able to read certain words on the charts which you did not introduce through a formal method. Ask them to point and say a word they recognize on the Word Charts. For example, your student may know the word <u>l</u>et because they have read it somewhere before. At this stage the student has been formally introduced to the <u>e</u> and <u>t</u> sounds, but not the <u>l</u>. Now is a good time to introduce the 'bright blue' <u>l</u> sound in column 41. Since this is a consonant, we can not say its sound in isolation. Instead, combine this new sound with ones the student already knows. Move to the Fidel and for example, tap out <u>l</u> , <u>a</u> and <u>p</u> to spell <u>lap</u>.

If the student is unable to read new words on the Word Chart, then move over to the Fidel, point to a new column and say it once. Then, point to it again, and have the student say it. Remember, if it is a consonant you must combine it with a vowel sound.

# Teaching Technique: Introducing a New Spelling

If you want to introduce a new spelling to the student, you may find the following technique useful. For example, if your students know the word fan and the word let, they have been given enough criteria for them to accurately spell the word laugh.

Start by separately tapping out the words fan and let on the Word Charts. If they have trouble saying either of those words, slow down and do it again. When they get it, go to the Fidel and tap the individual symbols of fan (f a n) and then let (l e t). Now, tap on the same l (as in let), the a (as in fan) and the f (as in fan). Have them say laf.

Now introduce the correct spelling of laugh. Tap on l (as in let), then under the same column in the Fidel as the a (as in fan), tap on the au spelling, then tap the f (as in fan). You have tapped out lauf. Make sure the student pronounces the word the same as before. Repeat the process, this time tap the gh in the same column instead of the f. Repeat the process, if your students are having difficulty reading the word laugh.

This exercise can be done for a wide range of new words. For words that are not on the Word Charts, you will be able to tap all the spellings in the English language using the Fidel.

# Teaching Technique: Introducing Diphthongs

A diphthong is formed by combining two sounds into one spelling. To see an example of one, look at column 16 on the Fidel. This column introduces a sound as in the first person I. As you can see this is combines the 'white' sound as in pot (column 5) with the 'pink' sound as in yes (column 40). Here is a technique which you may find useful when introducing these sounds.

Have the student find a word that has the 'white' sound, for example pot. Cover up the letter t only; the student should say po, cover up the p only; the student should say ot. Now, cover up both the p and the t until the student can isolate and pronounce the 'white' o properly. Now, move onto a word that has the 'pink' y, for example yes. Since the letter y in this word is a consonant, we can not pronounce it in isolation. Instead, tap the 'white' o, then tap the word yes. Have them say o-yes again until it sounds smoothly. Now, repeat this exercise, but this time cover the es. The student should be able to realize that he or she is blending the 'white' sound with the 'pink' sound together. They should be able to say the sound of the first person I. Have them repeat it until they say it smoothly with confidence. Now, you can introduce the correct spelling of the first person I by taping on it in column 16.

# Teaching Technique: Substitution Game

Teacher writes a word; <u>pop</u> (for example) and asks the student to read it. Then they write a second word; <u>pap</u> and asks the student read it. Next the teacher asks the student which letter do I have to change if I want to transform the first word (<u>pop</u>) into the second word (<u>pap</u>). This game can be continued with other words. For example:

- <u>pip</u>  »  <u>pep</u>
- <u>pep</u>  »  <u>pap</u>
- <u>pep</u>  »  <u>pup</u>
- <u>pop</u>  »  <u>pep</u>
- <u>pip</u>  »  <u>pop</u>
- etc.

The game can also be played with short simple sentences which gradually become more complex. For example, the teacher could:

- Write two sentences on the board:  <u>pop up</u>  »  <u>pep up</u>
- Next they would ask: "What word do you have to change to transform the first sentence into the second?"

# Words in Color Toolbox
## GAMES

# Pre-Reading Rhythm Game

### Materials:
- Pointer
- Cards or rods

### Prep time:
- 0 min.

### Level:
- Beginner

## Purpose:

To create an awareness that spaces between sounds can be expressed by spaces between objects.

## How to play:

The teacher taps a pattern on the table. For example:

The student then takes cards or rods and puts them in the same pattern.

## Variations:

- Question & Answer: The teacher taps, and then student taps the same.
- While working on a new sound from Chart 0, the teacher taps the table and student says the new sound. The game can be extended to include multiple sounds. For example, the table top and a book could be used, because they make different sounds when tapped. The table top would represent one sound and the book would represent another sound. If the student does not relate to the tapping, try having them jump. The teacher could say a sound, and the student would then jump. When the teacher says two sounds, the student jumps twice.

# Pre-Reading Listening Game

### Materials:
- NA

### Prep time:
- 0 min.

### Level:
- Beginner

### Purpose:
To create an awareness that words are made of several sounds.

### How to play:
The teacher asks the student if they can hear the sound <u>a</u> in the word <u>pat</u>, <u>pet</u>, <u>pot</u>, etc.

### Variation:
Instead of answering with "yes" or "no," the student could stand for "yes" and sit for "no."

# Repeating the First Consonant

**Materials:**
- NA

**Prep time:**
- 0 min.

**Level:**
- Beginner

## Purpose:

To create an awareness about the smooth transition between consonants and vowels in our speech.

## How to play:

The teacher uses a hand gesture to show the blend between consonant and vowels. For example, if introducing p, the teacher could have a closed fist for p and open their hand as they move to a. The teacher can start by mouth pa with the hand gesture, so the student can see a closed mouth with a closed fist, and an open mouth with an open hand. The student can then say the sound as the teacher gestures.

## Variation:

The teacher adds another consonant sound at the end and re-closes their fist as they say it. Then the student then has to follow along with the new gestures.

# Suzette's First Consonant Game

### Materials:
- Pencil and paper

### Prep time:
- 0 min.

### Level:
- Beginner

## Purpose:

To create an awareness of how consonants and vowels are blended while introducing the students' first consonant. This game is appropriate to play after the student is comfortable with the five vowels on Chart 0, and Reading Primer $R_0$.

## How to play:

The teacher says a sound, for example <u>a</u> as in <u>pat</u>. The teacher then says, "I am going to do something to this sound," then says, "<u>am</u>." The teacher asks what she did to the sound. The student may say, "You added a sound at the end." If they don't answer this way, the teacher can ask questions until the student understands what is different about <u>a</u> and <u>am</u>. Then the teachers asks, "Can you write it?" The student should be able to write <u>a</u>, but the <u>m</u> will likely be illegible squiggles. Now the teacher would write <u>m</u> and ask how many legs, and how many bumps it has. Once the student writes something that looks like <u>am</u>, they can read it to the teacher, and read it on the charts or Fidel.

The teacher can continue by blending <u>m</u> with the other vowels.

Introducing the first consonant in this way by saying it first, then writing it, makes sure students don't read <u>m</u> as "muh" or <u>p</u> as "puh."

# Continued...

> **Variation:**
>
> The teacher can carry on by asking the student to write sounds like <u>am</u>, <u>im</u>, <u>um</u> on the board, then ask them to erase the sound they say.

# First Consonant Game

**Materials:**
- Pencil and paper

**Prep time:**
- 0 min.

**Level:**
- Beginner

## Purpose:

To create an awareness about how vowels and consonants are blended, so that students don't begin to read with gaps or extra sounds between sounds.

## How to play:

The teacher says a long extended <u>a</u>, then says a long extended <u>m</u>. (<u>m</u> is a good first consonant because it can be extended.) The teacher then makes the shape with their mouth, but doesn't make the sound. Then the teacher says <u>a</u>, and mouths the sound for <u>m</u> but doesn't say it. Next the teacher mouths the sound for <u>a</u>, and says <u>m</u>. Finally, the teacher says the sounds in <u>am</u> together. The teacher can then write <u>am</u>, say <u>am</u>, and ask the student to read it.

## Variation:

The teacher mouths the sound, or the sound combination, and the student says the sound.

# Retention Game

### Materials:
- Imagination

### Prep time:
- 0 min.

### Level:
- Beginner +

## Purpose:

To explore words sign by sign, segment by segment, and sound by sound. This game will also help practice visualization, and therefore aid in retention.

## How to play:

Have the students close their eyes. Ask them to:
- See the word.
- See the first sign, the second, the third etc.
- See the first color, the next, etc.

## Variation:

Tell them a series of colors, and ask them what the next color is. Then ask, "What is the word?"

# The Transformation Game

### Materials:
- Pencil and paper

### Prep time:
- 1 min. to select and write start and end points.

### Level:
- Introduce after $R_1$

## Purpose:

To explore the algebraic properties of English.

## How to play:

The object of the game is to go from one word to another through a succession of changes, using only four operations, and making only one change at a time:

- (s) substitution (of one sound for another)
- (a) addition (of one sound at the beginning or end of a word)
- (i) insertion (of one sound within a word)
- (r) reversal (of the sounds of a word)

Give your student pairs of words and increase the difficulty and complexity of the challenges as the game develops. The basis for the game is not single letters but signs, each of which may contain several letters representing one sound. Each step must produce a legitimate English word. In most cases, there is more than one way to go from one word to another.

Note that subtraction is not permissible in the game, although it is obvious that it can be used for word formation. It would reduce the interest of the game by making almost all challenges too easy.

# Continued...

**Example: From at to sips**

$$at \begin{array}{c} \nearrow \\ \searrow \end{array} \begin{array}{c} it \xrightarrow{a} pit \xrightarrow{r} tip \xrightarrow{a} tips \\ pat \xrightarrow{r} tap \xrightarrow{s} tip \xrightarrow{s} sip \end{array} \begin{array}{c} \searrow \\ \nearrow \end{array} sips$$

In the beginning, don't insist on getting results, but rather make sure that the rules are clear and that your student understands what they are supposed to do. The transformation game is played throughout the Words in Color program.

**Variation:**

Instead of writing, try the game orally. Starting with pat, ask them: "How would this word sound with the ice blue one instead of the buff one?" (pet). Then ask what other changes they can make (one at a time) to arrive at pits.

# Evocation Game 1

### Materials:
- Word grid on board

### Prep time:
- First create the grid through another game. Play that game for as long as the students are interested.

### Level:
- Beginner +

## Purpose:

To explore sounds and practice relating sounds to spellings.

## How to play:

After developing a word bank on the board through another game, the teacher selects a secret word. The teacher asks which word they are thinking of, and gives one hint. For example, "My word has this sign at the beginning," and points to it on the Fidel. The students try to determine the secret word, and the teacher can give hints as they see fit.

## Variations:

- A student can choose the word and give hints to the rest of the class.

- From the word bank, the teacher erases one sound and asks the students to evoke the whole word.

# Evocation Game 2

*This game can be used to develop a word bank on the board.

### Materials:

- Signs written on paper
- Box or hat

### Prep time:

- 10 min. to write signs on small pieces of paper

### Level:

- Beginner +

## Purpose:

To create an awareness of the algebraic nature of English, and to experiment with algebraic transformations.

## How to play:

Start with a collection of signs in a box. Students pull signs from the box, and the teacher sticks them to the wall or board so everyone can see. The class can then make words, phrases, and sentences with the signs they see. After each word is evoked, a student can write the word on the board. When there are a couple of words on the board, the students can write sentences using the words.

## Variation:

Each student makes their own box of signs and writes down all the words they can make. They then trade boxes with their neighbor, and compare their lists.

# Evocation Game 3

### Materials:

- Fidel
- 1 or more word charts
- Word grid on board

### Prep time:

- First create the grid through another game (optional).

### Level:

- Beginner +

### Purpose:

To explore sounds and spellings by evoking words according to specific criteria.

### How to play:

The teacher opens her hand and shows it to the students. Then closes her hand and says: "I have a word in my hand. Do you know which one it is?" At this point it is not possible for the students to know. The teacher then says it has this many sounds and holds up a number of fingers corresponding to the number of sounds. Students try and determine what the word is.

Next, the teacher tells the students the word contains a sound and points to the sound on the Fidel, and the students try again to determine the word. The game continues with the teacher revealing clues until the students have determined with the word is.

The game can be played with the teacher focusing on the words on a specific chart or by starting with a grid of words.

There may be many words that fit the specific criteria. If the students guess a word that has a sound in the same spot, then she may tell them. Your word and my word have the same sound in this position, as she points to her finger.

# Continued...

### Variations:

- The teacher may change the type of clues given, such as:

    - Showing a number of fingers that correspond to the number of sounds in the word and saying, "My word looks like this." The teacher can then arrange their fingers so that the number of sounds in each syllable is visible.
        - This one is pink (teacher points to one of her fingers)
        - My word is on this chart – points to a chart

- The students can take turns being the teacher and choosing their own words.

# Point of View Game

### Materials:
- Pencil and paper (optional)
- Rods (optional)

### Prep time:
- 0 min.

### Level:
- Beginner +

## Purpose:

To explore words form many points of view: sounds, spellings, rhythm, beats, etc.

## How to play:

The teacher provides a word and asks questions about it:
- How many sounds?
- How many syllables/beats?
- Group the letters according to sounds. (Students could write the word and draw slashes or circles to separate the sounds.)

## Variations:

- Instead of answering by saying the number, the students could hold up a rod (a white rod for one, a red rod for two, etc.), by holding up their fingers, or by clapping, jumping, or touching their toes.

- The student can become the teacher and ask questions about a word of their choice.

# Anne Marie Claire's Dictation Game

**Materials:**
- Pencil and paper

**Prep time:**
- 0 min.

**Level:**
- Beginner +

## Purpose:

To practice visualization, spelling, and differentiating vowels from consonants.

## How to play:

The teacher dictates a word, phrase, or sentence. The students write the vowels on a piece of paper, but replace the consonants with a line, __. If the teacher says "thirsty," students write "__ i __ __ __ y." The teacher and students should agree before the game begins whether a sound like "th" should get one space or two. The students can then explain why they may have different answers.

## Variations:

- The students write the consonants and replace the vowel sounds with lines.

- The teacher says the word or sentence, and a pair of students comes to the board. The student on the left writes the vowels, and the student on the right writes the consonants. The rest of the class can decide if both answers on the board are correct.

# Word Pattern Game

### Materials:
- List of words (optional)
- Patterns and words sheet (optional)

### Prep time:
- 5 min. to prepare a list of words for game variation (optional)
- 10 min. to prepare a sheet of patterns and words (optional)

### Level:
- Beginner +

### Purpose:

To explore the difference between consonants and vowels, and to explore sound patterns.

### How to play:

The object of the game is to make as many words as possible that fit a given pattern.

First, the teacher puts a pattern on the board:

1. ● over line with ● ● below
2. ● ● ● over line with ● ● ● ● ● below
3. __ __ __ __ __

The line indicates the line on the Fidel that separates the vowels on the top from the consonants on the bottom.

In the first example, words include: <u>pit</u>, <u>pat</u>, <u>pot</u>, <u>pet</u>, <u>pop</u>, <u>pep</u>, etc.

When the students have come up with many answers, the teacher can then change the pattern by adding a dot, or changing the order of the dots. The teacher can do the pattern game until all the words on a particular chart are used.

# Continued...

### Variations:

- The teacher can put up two patterns and ask what the difference is between pattern 1 and pattern 2.

- The teacher can name the patterns (e.g. pattern 1, pattern 2, pattern 3). Then she can read a word and ask which pattern it belongs to.

- The teacher can give a list of words to the students. The students would then have to make a list of patterns that correspond to the words.

- The students can make the pattern, then they write a word, say it, read it etc.

- The teacher prepares a page with two columns. In the left column she writes patterns. In the right column she writes words. The students then match the pattern in the left column to the corresponding words in the right column.

# Definition Game

*This game can be used to develop a word bank on the board (in Variations).

### Materials:

- Word bank on board

### Prep time:

- First create the grid through another game. Play that game for as long as the students are interested.

### Level:

- Beginner +

## Purpose:

To practice associating written words with their meanings, and to practice grouping words.

## How to play:

This game starts with a word bank on the board. The teacher then provides a short description of one of the words. For example: "My word is something that you can cook with." Then the teacher asks which word it is. The students determine which of the words the teacher is talking about.

## Variations:

- The student can be the teacher and describe one word.

- Play the game in reverse to develop a word bank. The teacher can give a description, and the students can write the word.

# Little Piece of Paper Game

### Materials:
- Little pieces of paper (receipt roll works well)
- Hat or box

### Prep time:
- 0 min.

### Level:
- Beginner +

## Purpose:

To practice writing as well as reading without color.

## How to play:

This game is best suited for students using Reading Primers $R_0$ & $R_1$. Each person writes a word or a sentence on a piece of paper and puts it in a hat. A roll of receipt paper works well for this. The hat is passed and students take a piece of paper and read it out loud. Their neighbor can look to make sure it was read correctly.

## Variation:

One student would read the word and the others would write it in their notebooks. After they have written the word, they could be asked to write sentences using the word.

# Write What You Like Game

**Materials:**
- NA

**Prep time:**
- 0 min.

**Level:**
- Beginner +

**Purpose:**

To practice self-expression through writing.

**How to play:**

After warming up by pointing to sounds and words and sentences, students can write whatever they like.

**Variation:**

Students could then draw a picture relating to what they wrote.

# Color Dictation Game

### Materials:

- 1 or more word charts
- Fidel (optional)

### Prep time:

- 0 min.

### Level:

- Beginner +

### Purpose:

To create an awareness about the connection between color and sound, explore color and sound combinations, and practice decoding words.

### How to play:

The teacher walks around the classroom, selects a student, and stands behind them. When the teachers says the colors ("pale yellow, lime green"), then the student says the word ("us"). Words can be chosen from a word chart, or from the Fidel.

### Variations:

- A student can play the role of the teacher by selecting a classmate and saying the colors.

- Instead of saying the word aloud, the student whispers it to the teacher. The answer is kept a secret, so the teacher can say the same colors to multiple students.

# The Rod Game

**Materials:**
- 3 or more rods
- 1 or more word charts

**Prep time:**
- 1 min.

**Level:**
- Beginner +

## Purpose:

To practice decoding words as well as relating spoken words to written words.

## How to play:

Teacher places rods under three different words on the word charts. Rods can be adhered with blue tack. Students place rods on their table in the same arrangement as those placed on the word charts by the teacher. The teacher then says a word and the students hold up the corresponding rod. For example, if a yellow rod is under the word "stamps," the students should hold up their yellow rod when "stamps" is read.

Can be used to practice:
- 1 sign that has many spellings
- 1 spelling that has many signs

## Variations:

- Teacher puts five rods under different words and then reads four words. Students have to determine which word was not read.
- Teacher shows a rod and asks the students to read the word associated with that rod.

# The Challenge of the Day Game

### Materials:

- Pointer
- Cards or rods

### Prep time:

- 5 min. to decide sentence and write pattern on board

### Level:

- Beginner +

### Purpose:

To explore sounds, spellings, and sentence structure.

### How to play:

The teacher writes a sentence, and then organizes the sounds into a Fidel-type grid with vowels on top and consonants on the bottom. She then draws one space for each word in the sentence. If the students have already met ambiguities, it is a good idea to say the sounds on the grid. At the end of the day, the students can share their answers.

For example:

| a e o |
|---|
| p m s t n |

__ __ __ __

(Answer could be "Pam stamps on steps.")

### Variation:

Each day a different student can provide the Challenge of the Day.

# Text With Repeated Words

### Materials:
- Pre-written story

### Prep time:
- 10 min. to write original story, or 0 min. if story is already written

### Level:
- Beginner +

## Purpose:

To explore the concept of context, and to practice reading.

## How to play:

First, choose some words and work with them on the word charts and on the Fidel. Then introduce a written story to the class with those words in it. The text can be read more easily and more fluently, if students work on the words in advance.

## Variation:

Tell students there is a story with these words in it, and have them predict what the story is about. Then give them the story to read.

# The Secret Notebook

**Materials:**
- Student notebooks

**Prep time:**
- 0 min.

**Level:**
- Beginner +

## Purpose:

To practice self-expression through writing.

## How to play:

Each student has a secret notebook, and they can write anything they want in it every day. Once a week, they can read something to the class.

## Variation:

If students are very happy with their work, they can take a few minutes each day to read to a partner.

# Top Half Bottom Half Game

### Materials:

- Sheet of paper (optional)
- 1 or more word charts (optional)

### Prep time:

- 1 min.

### Level:

- Beginner +

### Purpose:

To explore the shapes of signs and words in order to improve decoding skills.

### How to play:

Teacher writes a word or a sentence on the board and then erases or covers up the bottom half of the word. The students then try to decode and read the word.

### Variations:

- To increase the difficulty, cover up the top half of the word.
- Use the color-coded word charts instead of the board to practice decoding color.

# Up, Down, Left, Right Game

**Materials:**
- Word grid on board

**Prep time:**
- First create the grid through another game. Play that game for as long as the students are interested.

**Level:**
- Beginner +

## Purpose:

To explore the meanings of words and experiment with sentence construction.

## How to play:

With an organized grid of words on the board, the teacher says one word and gives a direction. The student then says a sentence using all of the words in the line.

For example:

| | | | |
|---|---|---|---|
| pit | pat | pot | pup |
| sits | sip | sat | set |
| stop | steps | past | puppet |

If the teacher says "Pup. Down." The student could say, "The pup set the puppet on the chair."

## Variation:

Give opportunities for the class to change words in the grid. For example, if puppet has been read a few times, the class may be more excited if it is changed to monster. The class must change a noun to another noun, and a verb to another verb etc.

# Alain's Big, Little Space Game

**Materials:**
- 2 sheets of paper

**Prep time:**
- 1 min. to write 2 sounds on 2 pieces of paper

**Level:**
- Beginner +

## Purpose:

To create an awareness about how sounds are blended.

## How to play:

The teacher writes two sounds on two sheets of paper, for example <u>a</u> and <u>i</u>. Then the papers are given to two students who are standing at the front of the class, far apart from each other. The class says the sounds. Progressively the students move closer together and when they do, the sounds are said in succession more quickly until they are side by side and there is no pause between them when spoken.

## Variation:

After the above demonstration, each student writes a sound on a piece of paper (there can be more than one of the same sound). The students move around the classroom and find a partner. They read each other's sounds, then hi-five and say the blended sound.

# Alain's Practice Cards Game

**Materials:**
- 5+ word flash cards

**Prep time:**
- 10 min. + to make as many flash cards as needed

**Level:**
- Beginner +

## Purpose:

To practice decoding black-and-white words.

## How to play:

The teacher prepares word flash cards in black-and-white on one side, and black-and-gray on the other side. On the black-and-gray side, the sounds in the word alternate between black and gray.

| chicken | ch*ick*en |

The teacher shows the plain black-and-white side, and asks students questions about the word such as, "How many beats? How many sounds?" If the students can't agree, the teacher can show the black-and-gray side for a few moments and ask again.

For convenience, teachers can prepare these cards for each Word Building Table in the Reading Primer books and number the cards with the corresponding table number.

## Variation:

The teacher shows the cards upside-down, then asks the students to read the word, then write the word. The students can then trade papers with their neighbor and check their answer.

# Jacques' Overhead Word Game

*Depending on the technology available, this game can be adapted to posters or computer presentations.

### Materials:

- Overhead projector
- Word bank on overhead slide
- Paper with cut-out

### Prep time:

- 10 min. to prepare the overhead

### Level:

- Beginner +

## Purpose:

To create an awareness about specific ambiguities, or just to explore the necessary sounds and spellings.

## How to play:

On an overhead slide there is a grid of words. The teacher has a piece of paper with a window cut out of the middle to reveal words, or sounds. The words can be revealed one sound at a time, or one letter at a time, until the students can determine the word.

## Variation:

This game can be used to compare and contrast sounds and spellings. If the teacher wants to contrast the t in teach with the t in education, they can reveal teach first, then reveal only the t in education. Next, they can reveal tion and let the students begin determining the word.

# Spelling Games

*This game can be used to develop a word bank on the board.

### Materials:
- Wall charts

### Prep time:
- 0 min.

### Level:
- Beginner +

## Purpose:

To explore sounds and spellings, and practice writing.

## How to play:

The teacher asks students to find words on the wall charts that start with the same sound, and the same spelling. The students can be in teams, but they must take turns writing the answers. The teacher changes the challenge each round by asking the students to find other kinds of words. For example, to find words that have a certain sound in them, or to find words that have three sounds and start with a certain sound.

## Variation:

One student from each team can write their answer on the board. If two students from different teams write the same word, they both have to think of another possible answer. At the end of the game there will be a word bank on the board to play other games with.

# "Nym" Games

### Materials:
- Word cards (optional)

### Prep time:
- 10 min. to prepare word cards (optional)

### Level:
- Beginner +

## Purpose:

To explore the uses of synonyms, antonyms, and homonyms.

## How to play:

The teacher provides a word and asks the students to find:

> A synonym » spell it, use it in a sentence
> An antonym » spell it, use it in a sentence
> A homonym » spell it, use it in a sentence

## Variation:

The teacher prepares words on paper that can be paired as synonyms, antonyms, and homonyms. Each student gets a word, and is asked to find their synonym partner, then their antonym partner. If the cards don't pair up perfectly, and some students don't have partners, the class can determine what words their partners would have.

# Amazing Question & Answer Game

*This game can be used to develop a word bank on the board.

### Materials:
- Fidel

### Prep time:
- 0 min.

### Level:
- Beginner +

## Purpose:

To explore and practice using different spellings.

## How to play:

This game is played with two students on the Fidel. One student points to a spelling on the Fidel, for example ld, and the other student completes the word, such as would, should, could.

## Variation:

The student writes their answer on the board. This would generate a word bank on the board to play other games with.

# Fabienne's Famous Fidel Game

**Materials:**
- Pencil and paper or marker and whiteboard

**Prep time:**
- 0 min.

**Level:**
- Beginner +

## Purpose:

To create an awareness about the Fidel, and to explore sounds and spellings.

## How to play:

The teacher gives a sentence, then the student sorts the sounds and spellings into a Fidel-type grid. This means the vowel sounds will be arranged by sound on the top of the page, and the consonants will be arranged by sound on the bottom. The order of the sounds is not important, as long as the same sounds are grouped together, and vowels are on the top.

## Variation:

The student uses colored pencils or markers to match the Fidel.

# Vertical & Horizontal Game

### Materials:
- Fidel
- Wall charts (optional)

### Prep time:
- 0 min.

### Level:
- Beginner +

## Purpose:

For students to practice using multiple spellings of the same sounds, and multiple sounds for the same spelling.

## How to play:

In the Vertical Game, students make a sentence using words that include all the signs from one column in the Fidel. If the students haven't learned all the signs, the teacher can cover up the ones they haven't learned.

In the Horizontal Game, students make a sentence using words that have the same spelling from different columns.

## Variation:

To make the game easier, students can look for spellings in the word charts.

# Ambiguous Word Game

**Materials:**
- NA

**Prep time:**
- 0 min.

**Level:**
- Beginner +

## Purpose:

To create an awareness about ambiguous meanings, and to practice putting words in context.

## How to play:

The teacher writes a word with an ambiguous meaning and the student says a sentence for each meaning. For example, the teacher could write "spot." The student could then say, "There is a spot on my shirt. Can you spot Pat? Save a spot for me."

## Variation:

The student comes up with a list of ambiguous words they know then provides the context in a sentence.

# Word Chart Transformation Game

### Materials:
- Word charts

### Prep time:
- 0 min.

### Level:
- Beginner +

## Purpose:

To explore the algebraic nature of English.

## How to play:

Using the word charts, the teacher asks, "What do I need to do to change this word into that word?" If the students can't answer, the teacher can ask, "What is the same?" and cover up the parts of the word that are different. For example, if the words are pit and pot, the teacher would cover up i and o, then cover up p and t. This is a good setup to teach the conventional names given to word transformations (addition, substitution, insertion, reversal).

## Variation:

Two students can each point to a word while a third student determines how to transform one word into the other.

# Erase a Word Game

**Materials:**
- Word grid on board

**Prep time:**
- First create the grid through another game. Play that game for as long as the students are interested.

**Level:**
- Beginner +

## Purpose:

To explore words through deconstruction/reconstruction and to practice visualizing words.

## How to play:

After developing a word bank on the board through another game, the teacher erases the last sign in each word and asks the students what the word was. Another sign from each word is erased, and then students read what the word was.

The teacher continues erasing one sign at a time. Words that are erased can then be pointed out on the Fidel. ("What used to be here? Show me on the Fidel.")

## Variation:

Point to a sound on the Fidel, and have one or two students erase all instances of that sound from the words on the grid. Ask the rest of the class if they agree.

# Chart Exploration Game

**Materials:**
- All word charts
- Sticky notes

**Prep time:**
- 0 min.

**Level:**
- $R_2$ & $R_3$

## Purpose:

To explore the parts of speech, and practice grouping words.

## How to play:

With all of the charts on the wall, the teacher asks the students to find all the words that relate to: animals, the body, time, people, food, colors, places, actions, qualities, etc.

As the students find words that relate to the given topic, they can place sticky-notes next to them. Next, they can classify words (e.g. noun, verb, etc.) and make a sentence.

## Variation:

The teacher selects one word from the word charts and asks them to find all the other words that "go with" it. The students can explain why they grouped words together.

www.ingramcontent.com/pod-product-compliance
Lightning Source LLC
Chambersburg PA
CBHW040911020526
44116CB00026B/26